Y'all Have Sinned

How Blaming Others Is Not
A Winning Strategy

Eddie Huff

www.TotalPublishingAndMedia.com

TABLE OF CONTENTS

ACKNOWLEDGEMENTS

Eternal thanks to:

Phillip Mann, to whom I owe my eternal life, who as an 18 year old "Black Hippie/Jesus Freak" shared the Gospel of Jesus Christ with this lost, high on drugs, mess that I was, on so many late nights at Sambo's restaurant and persevered to lead me to Christ, despite being accosted and threatened by my friends.

Fred G. Walker, my first pastor and mentor, for taking an interest in and loving this lost Black, radical kid, teaching him what Christ's love and forgiveness is. I know your own children, at times, must have been puzzled and envious of the time and love invested in me. I will never forget those many evenings and hours of prayer and counselling in your converted garage/prayer room. Your life and lessons you taught, live on and made me who I am today.

John P. Lee, my second pastor and brother in the Lord who took me from the spiritual incubator to becoming a Man In Christ. You did not want me to leave but God has taken me on an incredible, world wide journey that you prepared me for. Wish you could still be here to see this work that you are a part of.

Karen Lafferty, the Queen of Youth With A Mission's (YWAM), "Musicians for Missions", who recruited me to Europe and made me her Prime Minister. It opened my eyes, my wife's and our children's to the entire world beyond where we live and the ride of our lives. Who knew that was just the start to travelling and seeing the world. Thank you "Your Highness." I know a great treasure awaits you on the other side.

Rev. Jim Jenkins, who knew when we were students 45 years ago we'd have experienced so much, meet again and have so much in common. God is Great!!

Finally, to all of my adopted brothers and sisters at Jesus Chapel, El Paso, Shiloh Baptist Church in Flower Mound, TX, Youth With A Mission Holland, and Germany. Thank you for the fellowship. We shared so much. You will always remain in my heart.

Finally and of course, to my wife Vickie and kids, what can I say; you are the best. I could not be more blessed.

PREFACE

It is interesting that it is said, "the truth hurts" while it is also said, "the truth will set you free." Is it possible the two' things can be true at the same time? We are going to find out in the pages ahead. I can only say everything you are about to read is the truth, and I am pretty certain it is going to initially "hurt" a number of people. If you have not been offended in the early reading, just hold on I am sure I will get to you. It is, in all honesty, not my intention to hurt or wound anyone, but I know some of the things dealt with will hurt some, simply because it may cause a paradigm shift in their thinking. Having said that, it is my greatest hope, the same truth which causes some pain, also heals and sets people free.

This writing, while mostly my views and opinion, contains historical fact, biblical fact, and political fact, all at once and together. It is my contention one cannot separate history, or the information, events and lessons of the bible, or politics, from one another. Well, you can, but it is like removing a major organ from the body and expecting to have a healthy body. Biblical events are history and have had a tremendous influence on history, and politics, and vice versa. It reminds me of the fallacy of separation of church and state. If by church you mean specific denominations or manmade decrees, as represented by one group's belief system comprised of human dogma, then yes, you can separate those from the state; but you cannot remove the Church as represented by faith or a belief system from the individual - and individuals comprise the State. This is what has been the aim of Atheists, to remove faith from how the nation is run, but Atheism is as much a faith or belief system as religion. A faith in the idea there is nothing beyond the natural, physical and visible world. This is considered a "closed system." In other words, there is no outside force which has any effect upon this "natural" world. Many try to deny this and pretend a lack of faith in a supernatural order behind the natural order is not a faith, but it is a belief system and therefore it is "a faith."

The late, and very gifted preacher Dr. S.M. Lockridge put God and creation this way: "God made something from nothing, put it nowhere and told it to stay there." The Atheist version of that would be: "Something came from nothing and made itself stay there." In other words, we are asked to believe that everything came from nothing, out of nowhere, of its own accord, and here we are today. Please tell me how believing this does not take as much or more "faith" than the Lockridge quote. Nevertheless Atheism is a belief system, faith or religion, in which man is the pinnacle of all intelligence, controls thinking and governments around the world, and this voids the entire idea of separation of church and state. It is merely the "church of naturalism" vs. the multitude of Christian churches and other faiths, believing in a supernatural reality, outside our own closed, natural system. Look at that, I have probably already offended someone. As Gerard Butler, playing the main character in the film "Law Abiding Citizen" said, "I'm just gettin' started."

I feel I should also say it is not my intent to present a deep scholarly work here. It was a few years after I attended university and seminary, when first I realized the true benefit of my education. It was not as much what I learned in the classroom, as it was that I learned how to question and where go, to do my own research, and to find the answers to my questions. The best teachers are not the ones who give you all of the answers, but the ones who make you ask the most questions and hunger to find those answers on your own.

Success of this book will not be measured by the reader accepting what I have to say, but rather the reader taking what is here, adding to it what they can find researching on their own, then taking that and making others hunger for more on their own.

Introduction
"YEAH RIGHT, GOD!"

S everal years ago, I worked as a concert promoter and tour manager and promoter for Christian and Gospel Music artists in Europe. In the fall of 1990, a few days before a set of Shirley Caesar concerts, I awoke in the morning and felt the Lord impress upon me that I was to preach at her concert. What I received was a message for "Black Americans," the descendants of African slaves.

For those who do not know who Shirley Caesar is, she is the Queen of Gospel having won 12 Grammys and numerous other awards as well as selling millions of records. Although I had preached and taught many times, in the US, Africa and Europe, this was so far out of nowhere, at first, I wondered if I was making this up. Then I was reminded of one of Bill Cosby's first monologues; "Noah." For the one person who has never heard this monologue it goes something like this.

Noah hears a voice saying, "Noah!"
Noah asks, "WHO IS That?"
He hears "it is, THE LORD Noah!"
Noah asks, "What do you want? I've been good."
The Lord says, "I want you to build an ark."
Noah says "Right, what's an ark?"
The Lord describes the ark and Noah says, "Yeah Right!"

This is exactly how I felt thinking I heard God tell me I was to preach at Shirley Caesar's concert instead of her. "YEAH RIGHT!!"

Understand, I had never even been to a Shirley Caesar concert, or met her, and she had no clue who I was. However, this overwhelming feeling came quickly and strong upon me would not leave. This was not a normal thing for me. In fact, I had only had this happen once before, a few years earlier when, out of the blue, I felt God telling me I was to take a team to Uganda. Five months later I found myself standing on the runway of Entebbe Airport, Uganda.

My job as tour manager was to stay out of sight and leave the ministry up to the artist- especially in the case of pastor Shirley Caesar who did ministry herself every night on the road, and at her home church.

Shirley Caesar, the Queen of Gospel, was and is a legend. What a crazy thought, but I could not shake it. As the date and evening approached, I could think of nothing else. I eventually realized the thought, like the Uganda calling, just might be crazy enough to really be God speaking.

The day came and that afternoon, as we were setting up the hall and preparing for the sound check, Shirley, her musicians and singers arrived. Introduced as the organizer of the event, I politely greeted them and discussed production and logistics, but said nothing about the message the Lord had given me. Later, as I happened to see Shirley alone, I approached her and explained I believed God had given me a special message for the audience that evening, and if she felt it was right, could she call me up on stage to deliver it. I added, because she did not know me and might not trust or think it was from God, that it was OK if she did not call on me and that I would leave it with her and God. She simply looked at me strangely, and said, "We will see."

The crowd that evening numbered between 1200 and 1500 people. They were mostly Black, U.S. military personnel and their families. They were packed into a small but nice concert theater in Kaiserslautern, Germany where they received hours of the finest gospel music and ministry on earth. I was just outside, in the back of the hall handling T-shirt and music sales thinking, "...should I have my head examined; what was I thinking? Who do you think you are to ask Shirley Caesar to turn over the preaching portion of her ministry to you?"

At the end of the musical portion of Shirley's ministry I heard her begin to speak to the people and breathed a sigh of relief, thinking, "Whew, it was just my imagination and not God." Just as I had that thought, I heard Shirley say, "A young man approached me earlier this afternoon and said he had a message from the Lord and asked if he could share it with you. If you are here young man, would you please come up and share with us." My heart began pounding and fear gripped me, but my feet headed for the stage. Gripped with a certain amount of fear and dread, I delivered that message.

Following the event, later that evening, members of Shirley's band came to me saying how amazing the message was and asked if I had cassette tapes, assuming I did this type of thing regularly. I had to tell them I don't normally do this and have NO tapes or books. The greatest affirmation, however, came the next morning at breakfast when Shirley Caesar herself came to me to tell me I had delivered a great message. She, in fact, asked me to share again the following evening. I thank God for Shirley Caesar and her humble and obedient heart to allow an unknown person to take over the ministry at one of her meetings, not knowing who I was or what I might say. What courage, what sensitivity. May she always continue to be blessed.

I believe the time is finally right for this message to be delivered to a broader audience, and while much is still focused on the descendants of African slaves, it is a message not only for "Black America" but for everyone. The heart of what you are about to read is essentially what I told the audience that evening in Germany. The message was simple but a mere skeleton of what I have learned and added in these pages, however, the core of the message is the same simple message. God has blessed the descendants of African slaves in America, BUT, we are squandering that blessing. It is more relevant today than it was years ago and I can only pray that those who have ears to hear will hear, and that having heard will act on what they have heard.

Chapter 1
WE HAVE SINNED

As I wrote in the introduction, there I was a few days from organizing and running concerts with Shirley Caesar when I received a message from God saying I was to preach at the end of her concert. Once I accepted the message, I asked God, "What do you want me to say? What is my message to be?" God directed me to the 9th Chapter of the Book of Daniel.

Following the death of Solomon, the nation of Israel split into two separate kingdoms with separate kings, priests and prophets. The northern kingdom was Israel and the southern was Judah. The southern kingdom was ruled by descendants of David while the northern kingdom would be ruled by whomever was powerful enough to take and retain the position. Although both kingdoms remained the chosen people of God, each sinned against God and was removed from the land of promise and dispersed to other lands. As a result, only the descendants of the southern kingdom are traceable as a people. In AD70 they too were displaced from the land and dispersed by the Roman emperor Titus.

Israel, the northern kingdom, was the first to fall as a result of their sin against God. They were taken captive by the Assyrians, and as was the practice of the Assyrians, they were dispersed and intermingled with captive people from other nations. These Jews, for the most part never returned to their homeland. The remnant who were left remained in an area known as Samaria. The Assyrians then also, brought people from various nations to intermingle with the remnant, resulting in the emergence of the Samaritans. A people and community which was not accepted as Jews or by the Judeans due to their intermingling of heritage and religion.

Then there was the southern kingdom of Judah. They too sinned against God. As a result of their sin, they fell at the hands of the Babylonians and were carried away to Babylon. However, unlike the northern kingdom, as was prophesied by the prophet Jeremiah, after 70 years in captivity by the Babylonians, Medes and Persians remnants of Judah returned to rebuild their homeland.

I was led to the ninth chapter of the Book of Daniel and here I found the prophet Daniel praying for his people. This prayer, however, did not begin as we would expect a normal prayer would. Daniel, a student of the writings of the earlier priests and prophets believed in their writings. He read, understood and believed the writings of the prophet Jeremiah: This is what the LORD says:

"When seventy years are completed in Babylon, I will come to you and fulfill my good promise to bring you back to this place," Jeremiah 29:10 NIV.

This is where Daniel and some people of faith, today, differ in their response. Many believers, especially those in so-called "Faith" or "Word of Faith" congregations interpret this as influencing God's will, by our proclamation of faith. Our job is to merely hold onto his word and promises, "BELIEVE" strongly enough, shut out any negativity, keep proclaiming it and God has to perform. Belief is essential, but often it has to be accompanied by action.

I am not saying salvation is based upon works, BUT an active life in Christ is evidenced by work, both physical and spiritual. I agree God can and often does do things without us, but much if not most of the time, He wants us involved. This may include prayer, fasting, giving, and forgiving, among other things. Remember, James said, "Faith without works is dead."

In the case of Daniel, he did not take the words of Jeremiah's prophecy for granted and bide his time. Instead he sought God in earnest for a return to their promised land. What jumped out at me the most prominently, and what I saw as a message to the descendants of African slaves, (particularly those who call themselves believers) was Daniel's seeking of God through confession. He cried out to God, "WE have sinned." Notice, Daniel did not say THEY have sinned, referring to his fellow Jews in captivity, but WE have sinned. Daniel was a righteous man and true servant of God; and although he understood and believed the prophecy, he opened his window facing Jerusalem and began confessing the sins of the nation as his own. He could have prayed, "Lord have mercy on us and forgive those sinners who have done this and that." No, he said, WE have sinned, WE have done 'this and that'. He could also have blamed the Babylonians and asked God to smite them, but he did not. He confessed the sins of his people as his own.

We saw an example of judgment and punishment of the entire nation before, in the 7th Chapter of the Book of Joshua. God judged and punished the entire nation for the sins of one man. I cannot definitively tell you why God did this, but it is clear God judges families, cities, nations and churches (denominations) for the sins of the few. I suspect it is to tell us we are (and he expects us to be) in this together. Yes, you are your brother's keeper.

Let's look at Daniel's Prayer

"¹Xerxes' son Darius, who was a Mede by birth, was made ruler of the kingdom of Babylon. ² In the first year of his reign, I, Daniel, learned from the Scriptures the number of years that Jerusalem would remain in ruins. The LORD had told the prophet Jeremiah that Jerusalem would remain in ruins for 70 years. ³ So I turned to the Lord God and looked to him for help. I prayed, pleaded, and fasted in sackcloth and ashes.

⁴ I prayed to the LORD my God. I confessed and said, "Lord, you are great and deserve respect as the only God. You keep your promise and show mercy to those who love you and obey your commandments. ⁵ We have sinned, done wrong, acted wickedly, rebelled, and turned away from your commandments and laws. ⁶ We haven't listened to your servants the prophets, who spoke in your name to our kings, leaders, ancestors, and all the common people. ⁷ You, Lord, are righteous. But we—the men of Judah, the citizens of Jerusalem, and all the Israelites whom you scattered in countries near and far—are still ashamed because we have been unfaithful to you. ⁸ We, our kings, leaders, and ancestors are ashamed because we have sinned against you, LORD. ⁹ "But you, Lord our God, are compassionate and forgiving, although we have rebelled against you. ¹⁰ We never

listened to you or lived by the teachings you gave *us through your servants the prophets.* [11] *All Israel has ignored your teachings and refused to listen to you. So, you brought on us the curses you swore in an oath, the curses written in the Teachings of your servant Moses.* **We sinned against you.** [12] *So you did what you said you would do to us and our rulers by bringing a great disaster on us. Nowhere in the world has anything ever happened like what has happened to Jerusalem.* [13] *This entire disaster happened to us, exactly as it was written in Moses' Teachings.* LORD *our God, we never tried to gain your favor by turning from our wrongs and dedicating ourselves to your truth.* [14] *So you were prepared to bring this disaster on us.* LORD *our God, you are righteous in everything you do.* **But we never listened to you.**

[15] *"Lord our God, you brought your people out of Egypt with your strong hand and made yourself famous even today.* **We have sinned and done evil things.** [16] *Lord, since you are very righteous, turn your anger and fury away from your city, Jerusalem, your holy mountain. Jerusalem and your people are insulted by everyone around us because of our sins and the wicked things our ancestors did.* [17] *"Our God, listen to my prayer and request. For your own sake, Lord, look favorably on your holy place, which is lying in ruins.* [18] *Open your ears and listen, my God. Open your eyes and look at our ruins and at the city called by your name. We are not requesting this from you because we are righteous, but because you are very compassionate.* [19] *Listen to us, Lord. Forgive us, Lord. Pay attention, and act. Don't delay! Do this for your sake, my God, because your city and your people are called by your name."*

Daniel 9:1-19

The Case of Black America

In the case of Black America, WE have sinned. While I could go into a litany of sins, there are two major sins which I believe have led to the others - which I will call manifestations or consequences. Those two sins are ingratitude and unforgiveness. Unforgiveness being the most grievous of the two.

This is where I believe "Black America" must begin its road to real recovery and entrance into the fullness of things God has for His people of color, and the world as a whole. I believe some, if not many, will think and say I am a race traitor or label me self-hating for pointing these things out. I assure you I love my people and although I am mixed-race, I consider myself truly "black and proud." This pride is the source from which I write. I am disappointed Black America has accepted mediocrity, lies, deceit and scraps from the table of wicked men, black and white. It is my belief, until we as a people see and confess OUR sins, nothing will change.

Ingratitude

When I spoke to the audience back in 1990, I spoke of all the achievements and accomplishments of Black Americans in our short history, in America. I spoke of the influence Black culture has had on our nation and the world, in fashion, food, music, sports, the vernacular, and so much more. Think for a moment about the impact Black American culture has had on this nation and the world. I have yet to mention what was accomplished in the areas of science and medicine. Nevertheless, in-spite of the major accomplishments and influences of Black Americans (not to mention the accumulation of wealth) the focus remains on the negative - what we DON'T have instead of what we DO have. The ingratitude is astounding.

In Acts 17:26-27 it says: " *And He has made from one blood every nation of men to dwell on all the face of the earth, and has determined their pre-appointed times and the boundaries of their dwellings, so that*

5

they should seek the Lord, in the hope that they might grope for Him and find Him, though He is not far from each one of us."

While other races and nations have been recognized for their rich history and contributions to civilization, when black anthropologists and apologists make discoveries from early "Black Civilizations" as rich and important, they are too often selling mediocrity and in other cases, just plain myth. While we may come from humble beginnings, and not have an ancient history which stands out as something worthy of shouting about, our history should not be defined by what we were rather what we have become. It is our recent success and future potential (in spite of our past) which should make us proud and inspire us to build upon. In 1990 I told the crowd in Germany to look at our impact on modern society as an example of God's working and our importance in the world. There is so much richness and greatness to be seen.

What is seen daily in the news and championed in many venues today, however, is not greatness and achievement. It is our sexuality, foul language, failure at marriage and family, the crime and violence in our communities. They focus on high abortion rates, a reliance on and demand for social service programs – free welfare, free housing, free education and free medical care - free, free, free and freer.

We are also seen as ungrateful and always asking for more.

I wake up most mornings to the "NFL Today" show. Most days I hear some black football player demanding to be the highest paid at their position. How much is enough? Must it be more than the last guy? They say ten to thirty million dollars a year is not enough because someone else has more. Meanwhile, these same people complain and become activists for the less fortunate of our race, blaming the non-black culture for black failure. In the NBA we see the same thing. Where is the gratitude, humility, work ethic and a giving heart? Despite making millions of dollars these players along with their NFL top earners complain about the country, the president, political parties and the government not doing enough to help poor black families.

In 2008 CNBC did a special series called "The Rise of The Newbos." "Newbos" stands for New Black Overclass. The series highlighted the year 2007 in which black athletes, entertainers and "Hip Hop" artists earned over $4.5 Billion dollars. Consider $4 Billion $500

Million dollars for a moment. I thought about Hurricane Katrina just two years earlier and how it devastated the poor black neighborhoods of the New Orleans, "Lower 9th Ward, where 5000 homes were flooded. Many black entertainers, athletes and others attacked George W. Bush for not caring about "those people", yet how much of those athletes and entertainers' $4.5 billion do you suppose went to rebuilding the devastated homes in the Lower 9th Ward of New Orleans? Today many, if not most of the homes remain unrepaired. Devastated homes remain and empty lots encompass spaces where homes once stood. Apparently, it was much easier to attack George W. Bush than to write a check or start a rebuilding project.

Imagine if the "Newbos" just tithed (gave 1/10th) of their income to rebuilding New Orleans, in one year they would have contributed $450,000,000. To make it plain, if they rebuilt 5000 homes at $100,000 a piece, it would total $500,000,000. In other words, one year's tithe could have rebuilt all but 50 of the 5000 homes - which far exceeds what they were valued at prior to hurricane Katrina. In addition, in just another five weeks they could have paid for the additional 50 homes. Basically in 13 months they could have rebuilt the most devastated part of New Orleans. But no! It was easier for them to complain and blame the president and the government than to take responsibility for rebuilding a community they apparently cared about. The added benefit of doing it themselves is they could have overseen the work and made sure their dollars were not spent by corrupt politicians and greedy bureaucrats.

This is a prime example of what ingratitude leads to. Rather than thanking God for what is received, and responding to his calling to share these blessings, they seek more and more for themselves as they attack others for not doing anything about the needs of the less fortunate.

I recall watching the news just a few years later, before Hurricane Rita hit south Texas and much of the gulf coast. A news report has haunted me till this day, when a news person found a large, obese, black woman, sitting on a curb outside her home. The concerned reporter asked her if she should not be seeking shelter or escaping the area before the storm hit. The lady's response was as follows. "All I know is somebody needs to get me out of here as soon as possible." This lady had no inkling of self-preservation or initiative. In her mind it was someone else's responsibility to save her life; her responsibility was to sit there and wait for someone else to do their job.

I did not know whether to be angry or saddened by her attitude. What could so damage a person's view of life as to totally give up all efforts toward self-preservation and responsibility? What is worse is this lady was and is not alone in this damaged mentality. These are the crippling effects of an ungrateful culture. Ungrateful to God, ungrateful to a nation and ungrateful to fellow citizens. Black people have been taught and bought into the narrative, of someone owes us something, it's not our own actions which produce results positive or negative. Once this thinking takes hold of a people, they are easily enslaved and manipulated.

Unforgiveness

The second, and as I said before, the more serious sin is unforgiveness. Unforgiveness leads to a "root of bitterness", a root which leads to nothing but bad outcomes. We will look at the issue of slavery in depth later, but unforgiveness over slavery appears to be the root cause of bitterness by descendants of African slaves in America. We are led to believe the period of slavery is the cause of all the ills in Black communities. When we move beyond slavery, we are presented with the period known as "Jim Crow." Both of these were dark periods, yet there are those who cannot, or will not, move beyond these with forgiveness. I say, however, we as a people, cannot and will not progress and fully inherit what God intends for us until we forgive past wrongs and injustices.

As I stated in the intro, this book is primarily for "Believers." As such there are certain biblical truths, (non-believers may call them "Universal Laws") which I believe mankind must live by.

One of those is found in Matthew 6:15:

> *"But if you do not forgive others their sins,*
> *your father [in heaven] will not forgive your sins."*

This verse is about as clear as it gets. IF YOU DO NOT FORGIVE! It is my belief, the descendants of African slaves cannot expect anything from God UNTIL they actively forgive slave-traders, slaveholders, their descendents and what we call institutionalized racists for past sins.

Chapter 2

WHAT YOU MEANT FOR EVIL

A frican slaves in America and their early descendants took great solace in comparing their plight to the Hebrew people enslaved in Egypt. Many of the early "Negro Spirituals" were about the Hebrew Children. Even the 70s Rastafarian song "Rivers of Babylon" referred to the captivity of the Hebrews in Babylon. The descendants of African slaves in the U.S. and the Islands saw a likeness of their plight to the plight of the Jews.

Early on, this likeness brought hope to the oppressed. In looking at the plight and eventual outcome for the Jews, slaves and those who suffered under "Jim Crow," believed their cries would be heard by God and He would deliver them from their suffering and bondage. This comparison and relating of bondage, suffering, hope for freedom and prosperity prevailed in the black community into the 60s, at which time something changed.

I do not think the parallels between Jews of old and descendants of slaves are coincidental, or of little meaning. I am convinced there is a parallel, a parallel which was lost in the 60s.

Joseph

Almost every child in the western and middle eastern world knows the story of Joseph and his brothers. In the west, I am afraid, this story has deteriorated to making more of his "coat of many colors" and a children's story than the heart of the message, which I believe has been lost. There is so much richness in every aspect of Joseph's story, with aspects and parallels which apply to the descendants of African slaves and lessons which should have been learned.

Joseph was not the oldest, strongest or smartest of his brothers. He did, however, believe he was favored by God. He let his brothers know this. His brothers saw this, were jealous and hated him for it. What did his brothers do? They conspired and sold him into slavery in a foreign land.

11

Let's jump forward, say about 3200 years. West African tribes jealous and hateful of other tribes and individuals entrapped and sold their brothers into slavery in a foreign land. Hmm, sound familiar? Once in the foreign land Joseph distinguished himself as a special servant and rose to become the most gifted and trusted of all the servants. There he was considered more than a servant, but rather manager of all the owner had. Similarly, black Americans grew to become good workers and trusted servants in their new home.

Native Americans were the first to be put to work as servants on plantations, however African slaves were preferred. They proved to make better servants because of their endurance and hard work. I am not saying I thought this was right or a good system. I am just stating the facts as they were. Joseph was the best servant in Potipher's house and Africa slaves were the best in this house called America.

Let's continue the comparison and contrast. Joseph was sold into slavery by his brothers. Do you hear Jews blaming the Egyptians for buying or trading in human chattel? No. Nor are Jews asking for reparations for the 400 years they were enslaved and mistreated at the hands of the Egyptians. Descendants of Africans sold into slavery by their brothers are admonishing, blaming and seeking reparations.

Joseph rose to the head of Potiphar's house and was essentially free. Descendants of African slaves received their freedom and rose to prominence following the war of the states. Joseph went from the head of Potiphar's house to an Egyptian prison. Descendants of slaves, many of whom took very prominent positions in the south were essentially imprisoned, socially and politically, through Jim Crow laws.

In some ways, Jim Crow laws were worse than slavery, as I am sure the Egyptian prison was worse than being a servant in Potiphar's house. As slaves, many if not most, were fed, clothed, housed and taken care of. The problem was a lack of freedom and self-determination. Regardless of how well they were taken care of, there was no education, freedom to establish a family, freedom to come and go or to do what they wanted to do.

I believe Jim Crow in many ways, was worse, because former slave owners were no longer responsible for the upkeep of the now "freed" slaves. Former slaves endowed "unalienable rights" were not much, if any, better than when they were slaves. They now had to survive on their own with few attainable rights and with limited freedoms. In many ways freed American slave's lives were worse post emancipation, as (I believe) were the lives of Egyptian prisoners.

Joseph was eventually released from prison and lived to become the second most powerful man in Egypt. Similarly, the descendants of African slaves have become the second most powerful race in America. This culminated with the election of Barack Obama as President of the United States. Oppressed, enslaved, dispersed and often facing extinction, Jews have suffered multiple outrageous fortunes throughout history. Each of these sufferings, however, was a result of God's judgement - it was also God's grace and mercy which reestablished them. I have presented just a few of the parallels between the Jews and black Americans, now I want to discuss the differences.

First, how Jews look upon those who oppressed and mistreated them in the past. Although the Egyptians, Assyrians (Syrians), Babylonians (Iraqis), Persians (Iranians) enslaved and mistreated the Jews you do not hear them complaining or constantly blaming them for their ills. Nor do you hear them seeking reparations. Russia's Pogroms, Germany's Holocaust and other European actions against Jews are remembered but not trumpeted or unswervingly reiterated. I am sure someone will remind me of reparations to the Jews for the Holocaust. I forgotten, BUT those reparations were for tangible things stolen from the Jews, be it land or other property, not intangibles such as how great Jews might have been or what they may have accomplished were it not for the Holocaust.

Each time the Jews received God's help and were released from their plight, they worked and rebuilt their prosperity. They did not wait for others to take pity on them, or to give them handouts. They worked for it, fought for it, rebuilt it and in some cases recovered what was lost. It is evident, as told in the story of Joseph, but black Americans seem to have totally missed the message.

When Joseph attained his position in Egypt, he did not think it was about him, his suffering OR his success. He saw the greater purpose. When he revealed himself to his brothers, they became afraid and expected Joseph to exact vengeance against them. Joseph, however, told them something interesting. In Genesis 45:4-7 Joseph reveals himself:

> *"⁴ Then Joseph said to his brothers, "Come close to me." When they had done so, he said, "I am your brother Joseph, the one you sold into Egypt! ⁵ And now, do not be distressed and do not be angry with yourselves for selling me here, because **it was to save lives that God sent me ahead of you.** ⁶ For two years now there has been famine in the land, and for the next five years there will be no plowing and reaping.⁷ But **God sent me ahead of you to preserve for you a remnant on earth and to save your lives** by a great deliverance."* (NIV)

His brothers apparently did not really believe Joseph, because he had to once again assure them he had no intention of doing them harm. In Genesis 50:15-21:

> *"¹⁵ When Joseph's brothers saw that their father was dead, they said, "What if Joseph holds a grudge against us and pays us back for all the wrongs we did to him?" ¹⁶ So they sent word to Joseph, saying, "Your father left these instructions before he died: ¹⁷ 'This is what you are to say to Joseph: I ask you to forgive your brothers the sins and the wrongs they committed in treating you so badly.' Now please forgive the sins of the servants of the God of your father." When their message came to him, Joseph wept. ¹⁸ His brothers then came and threw themselves down before him. "We are your slaves," they said. ¹⁹ But Joseph said to them, "Don't be afraid. Am I in the place of God?²⁰ **You intended to harm me, but God intended it for good to accomplish what is now being done, the saving of many lives.** ²¹ So then, don't be afraid. I will provide for you and your children." And he reassured them and spoke kindly to them."* (NIV)

Most people around the world know the story of Joseph and most know he did not exact vengeance on his brothers. The phrase, "you intended to harm me, but God intended it for good", or "what you meant for evil God meant for good," is very well known and often repeated. However, the most powerful phrase in this exchange is one I fear is overlooked. "TO SAVE MANY LIVES!" This cannot be overlooked. There was a purpose and Joseph saw the purpose. He saw himself as part of a much bigger plan. If there is one overarching message I can give to my black brethren, it would be to "get over ourselves". To see ourselves as a piece in a much bigger picture.

President Kennedy's inaugural speech of 1961 is one of, if not the best ever delivered. I don't know what happened in the last 68 years, but we have lost the most memorable line of his speech. "Ask not what your country can do for you, ask what you can do for your country." As a nation, and particularly as a race, black Americans appear to have completely abandoned that ideal. In its place we see a self-absorbed, selfish, ungrateful, bitter people. It is more like, "ask not what you can do for your country, ask what your country can do for you." What your country, your state, your city, your neighbor, what anyone can do for you.

I should not have to say this, but I feel compelled to. I am not speaking to every last member of my race. There are many who still work hard and do care for this nation and other people who are truly in need, but too many now look to others for what they can get from them, instead of looking for what they can give to others. Descendants of African slaves were at one time a very caring and giving people. We looked out for our families, our neighbors, our communities and yes, even the families of those whom we served. We cooked for, we cleaned up after, and cared for these families, often raising their young children and caring for their elderly.

I do not believe the self-absorbed, bitter and unforgiving spirit I speak of is a natural or inherent attribute, any more than I believe Black People are naturally dumb, lazy and criminally inclined. This behavior has been taught and learned; conditioned if you will. In the next several chapters I will show how we got from there to here.

15

Chapter 3

FALSE PROPHETS

B lack Americans, descended from African slaves, should understand what I revealed in Chapter 2. A few black Christians and ministers may recognize the similarity in the story of Joseph to that of black Americans. Unfortunately, many and I fear most today do not. The more we have prospered as a people, the farther we appear to have come from understanding God's lessons.

Why is this the case? Let's take a look.

When the Jews left Egypt for the "Promised Land," right from the beginning there were many who did not believe in the journey. Something that never ceases to amaze me is the story of the Jews and their flight from Egypt. No, I am not amazed by the parting of the "Red Sea," the drowning of the Egyptians, or even the many judgements brought upon the Egyptians, which the Jews escaped. While those are amazing occurrences, what I am amazed by is how just a few weeks later the Jews were already upset at being in the wilderness. Never mind that they were free and that God had done many miracles to free them. They contemplated going back, speaking fondly of what they had left behind.

As a pampered city dweller myself, I understand that camping out is not an easy thing to adjust to. In the two or three times in my life that I have camped out, I was not a real fan until I got used to it. Camping long term with a few hundred thousand others, would take some adjustment. However, I do think that camping out and putting up with certain hardships would be preferable to being whipped, being at the mercy of slave drivers, and periodically having my firstborn child killed just for being a boy. These would be worth suffering the hardship.

However, seeds of doubt planted and watered by certain members of the Exodus festered and grew. If you will remember from Exodus 12, some Egyptians and other non-Jews were allowed to join in the Exodus (Ex. 12:37,38). I have to wonder what influence some of these may have had upon the Jews, helping to create and nurture the doubt as they journeyed into the wilderness. I suspect the people must have had some help in second guessing their decision.

The fear and doubt began almost immediately, when the Jews hit their first obstacle, the Red Sea. I have to give them that one, as I probably would have freaked too in that situation. However, only a few weeks after God had miraculously delivered them through the Red Sea and destroyed their enemy, they began grumbling and complaining about the living conditions, the water and the food supply.

The cries began, "God brought us out here to kill us." Better the pots of meat in Egypt that this CRAP!" *Exodus 16:3 EHV* (Eddie Huff Version)

How quickly they were ready to give up their freedom rather than endure hardship and work for the hope of a better life. Again, as with the Jews, after emancipation there were many ex-slaves that missed being taken care of as slaves, as opposed to the struggle which ensued in order to live free.

Moses sent 12 scouts out ahead to check out the land they would eventually settle in. When they returned there were 10 scouts that were ready to give up and only two who believed this was more than they could have hoped for. Because the people believed the 10 negative voices, the Jews wandered around in the desert for another 39 plus years. An entire adult generation died without ever seeing the promised land because they refused to have faith that they, with the help of their God, could overcome the obstacles (giants, fortified cities and strong armies) and be victorious.

In the same manner, for the last 50-60 years, black America, has listened to the same unbelieving, faithless and cowardly voices of negativity. Yes, different time and different people but the same "we can't do this, it's too hard," message. A message that to believe in a God who can and will deliver us to the promised land is foolish and we should not listen to those who would have us trust in Him. Like the Jews, the result has been a race of people wandering around in the desert of despair, without hope or vision.

We have had our own Jannes, Jambres and others, who opposed Moses and led the people to worship other Gods, keeping the people from entering into the promises of God. We have also had our own Joshuas and Calebs who saw a land of promise and saw us victorious over the giants that had to be conquered to possess it. Unfortunately, we have also had our 10 spies that have reported nothing but negativity and why we cannot win and possess the promised land. This is why I believe we as a people languish and struggle. It is not the forces from outside the community, rather the faithless and negative forces within which betray us at every step.

The people listened to these faithless voices and spent 40 needless years in the wilderness. I guess they finally got tired of wandering aimlessly waiting to be fed, and felt it was time to rise up and take what had been promised. This could not happen, however, until the negative voices died. It was when the people were ready to follow new leadership, one of faith, hope and promise at whatever cost, they finally entered in and possessed what was promised long before.

Since the Emancipation Proclamation, we have had a look into the Promised Land. The faithless, cowardly and self-serving have made us look at the giants instead of the promises of God. We have focused on slavery, Jim Crow, segregation, political parties, unjust laws, banks, finance companies and on and on as giants - and listened to the voices of wicked, lazy, corrupt and feckless men and women who call themselves leaders of our communities. One of the most feckless and faithless voices has been the "Black Church." Pastors and so-called preachers who have involved themselves more in controlling the sheep than feeding and leading them. They have sold out to politicians, parties, unions, and any other entity that will give them power and prestige. Instead of leading the people to freedom and prosperity, they have and continue to lead them as sheep to be fleeced. They conspire with politicians white and black, to keep the people wandering in the desert.

We had our Joshua, Caleb and mighty men. Frederick Douglas, Booker T. Washington and Marcus Garvey were three such men. They pointed the way but the traitors within undermined them and eventually turned the people against them, particularly Booker T. Washington. They did this by re-writing and misrepresenting who these men were and what they stood for. These three were the first to promote "Black Power." These three were like minded and had great influence. At the time these three men lived, black business, influence and standing grew greatly. After them it waned.

The rise of the Niagara Movement, and the NAACP with their leadership began the erosion of the memory of the mighty men of color. They were replaced by those like W.E.B. DuBois, and William Monroe Trotter.

Chapter 4

JUDAS GOATS

I n the 18th Century the so-called "Age of Enlightenment," also known as the "Age of Reason" expanded its influence upon the world, taking over thought in Europe and even influencing segments of American thought, particularly our elite universities. This movement which affected learning and thought about science, philosophy and religion, made its way to America in the latter part of the 19th Century. While much of the new intellectualism in the areas of science, medicine and economics, was a benefit, humankind and its elevation of man's intellect over the "wisdom from above," ushered in a secularization of society. Until then, "The Church," be it from Rome, Germany or England, had been the major influence on government and society.

I do have to say here that the state of "The Church," in Europe, at least the main denominations, was such that it deserved the rejection. Both major denominations, Catholic and Protestant, were more about power and wealth than the power of God and His Word.

In his 1882 book, "The Gay Science," Friedrich Nietzsche made the claim, "God is dead and we have killed him." In this proclamation, Nietzsche announced the death of a Judeo-Christian God, the faith(s) associated with Him, and the triumph of "The Enlightenment." In Nietzsche's mind the post-modern "enlightened" thinkers had proven there was no longer a need for God and the belief system surrounding Him. With the thought was that there was NO god or supernatural being or power beyond the physical universe, most "enlightened" thinkers celebrated the death of Christianity in particular.

Darwin and Natural Selection

One of the enlightened ones was Charles Darwin. In 1859 Darwin released his seminal work commonly known as the 1859 book, *"On the Origin of Species"*. The reason that I say, "commonly known as," is the fact that this is not the real title of the book, at least not the actual entire title of the book. Most of you will be shocked to learn that the actual full title of Darwin's book is:

"On The Origin Of Species By Means Of Natural Selection Or The Preservation of Favoured Races In The Struggle For Life."

That is the true full title of Darwin's book that changed science and education till this day. Now somehow one half of the title mysteriously disappeared when I was studying about Darwin's theory of evolution, in science class. I suspect 99% of those reading this missed that as well.

When I first read the words "the preservation of favoured races," I thought this must be someone's joke or a prank. As I began looking into this, no matter where I looked, I found the actual entire title, and it said the same thing, "OR the preservation of favoured races in the struggle for life."

Doing a bit more checking, I learned Darwin's family members were Eugenicists. Eugenics is the belief in promoting the multiplication of certain desirables of human society (the strong and intelligent) and the extermination of the undesirables (the weak and unintelligent).

The word "eugenics" was coined in 1883 by the English scientist Francis Galton, a cousin of Charles Darwin, to promote the idea of perfecting the human race by, as he put it, getting rid of its "undesirables" while multiplying its "desirables" -- that is, by encouraging the procreation of the social Darwinian "fit" and discouraging that of the unfit.

In Galton's day, the science of genetics was not yet understood. Nevertheless, Darwin's theory of evolution taught that species did change as a result of natural selection, and it was well known that by artificial selection a farmer could obtain permanent breeds of plants and animals strong in particular characteristics. Galton wondered, "Could not the race of men be similarly improved?"[1]

In addition to Galton, other members of Darwin's family were involved in the eugenics movement. Charles Darwin's son, Leonard, was the president of the first International Congress of Eugenics., and another son, George, promoted birth control among the lower class. They sought to lower, if not halt the reproduction of the so-called unfit.

In today's politically correct world Progressives and evolutionary scientists are loathed to discuss or reveal certain truths and facts. One of those is Darwin's Eugenicist thoughts and relations. They tell us that Darwin was not a Eugenicist and did not hold to these ideas, but in his later work, *"The Descent of Man,"* in 1871, he put forth that racial extermination has benefitted human evolution and brought mankind to where it was then. He further suggested that Caucasians aka white people, are superior to other races, particularly Africans and Aboriginal Australians.[1]

It is clear Darwin did, in fact, have Eugenicist leanings, if not an outright belief in it. What is also clear is that Darwin's influence combined with "Post Modern" atheism have led to many of the modern sociological ideas and outcomes. Sadly, those outcomes are not good ones, especially for black Americans.

The Darwinian view of life, eventually crept into the mainline churches, developing the thought, we today call, "Liberal Theology." Black America and the Black Church, for the most part was left out of this movement in its early days, mainly because the institutions of higher learning and mainline denominations did not accept them into membership, and frankly, they were a target for elimination. They did not, therefore, have the exposure to this new intellectualism or much mainline denominational dogma to reject. The newer and smaller, white denominations that did accept and reach out to the slaves and their descendants, offered a message of freedom and hope for their members. The Methodists, Episcopalians, Quakers and some Roman Catholics among them, believed in the equality of all mankind, had fought for abolition and sought to bring these new believers into the fold.

Later in the 19th Century these institutions of higher learning began to accept black students. Some, if not most of these black students became affected, or is it infected, by the intellectualism and a rejection of biblical faith. Among some of the "enlightened" black folks were three gentlemen, W.E.B. (William Edward Burghardt) DuBois, William Monroe Trotter and Archibald Grimke. All three were very intelligent, educated men who attended Harvard University. The three also lived in and were influenced by Boston and Harvard society. Of the three only Grimke was born into slavery, while Trotter and DuBois were not.

DuBois, however, was the only one of the three to not have either a forefather or foremother born into slavery. His influence, ironically, became the one that has affected mainstream black thought race and social activism, today, more than that of anyone else.

All three men attended and had their worldview shaped by their time at Harvard. DuBois, however, was not only influenced by his time at Harvard, where he was the first black person, to receive a Doctorate degree, he also spent time at the University of Berlin (Germany) where he was exposed to much more of the "Post Modern, Naturalism," which was essentially anti-God. When I think of DuBois, the German "thinkers," and intellectualism as a whole, I am reminded of the Apostle Paul's biblical warning, "professing themselves to be wise, they became fools." Romans 1:22 (KJV)

While black Americans and black people worldwide continued to be a very spiritual people, there were those including DuBois, Trotter and others who worked hard to change that or use it to their own benefit. Later we will look at who and what those influences were that have attacked and changed the thought pattern of the descendants of African slaves.

In addition to their time at Harvard the three men mentioned above shared one other notable characteristic, each one was opposed to the teachings and influence of Booker T. Washington. Grimke actually joined Washington and his efforts later on, but the other two opposed him vigorously. It was hard for these "highly educated", intellectuals to perceive that someone like Booker T. Washington, who came from poverty as a slave, with poor, uneducated parenting and what we would call a vo-tech diploma, could offer anything of value to black Americans toward their progress. To them, Washington and his ever-growing influence had to be stopped.

We will discuss Washington in greater detail a bit later but for now we will discuss the uniting principle of these men. All three believed that the progress of elevating the former slave to a place of equality and prominence was moving much too slowly. They believed and taught, in fact, that the way things were going in the south with Jim Crow laws, America could retreat back into a time of oppression and slavery for black Americans.

In 1905 Trotter and DuBois formed the Niagara Movement, specifically to counter the influence of Booker T. Washington. They believed in social protest and agitation against the social and political status quo. Trotter and DuBois believed social agitation was the quickest means by which to reach equality for black Americans. Demand it and use protests and social unrest, strikes, etc. to achieve this goal. Their agitation became so violent, particularly Trotter's, that they at one point started a riot at a location where Booker T. Washington was to give a speech. As a result of the growing violent direction of the Niagara Movement, Dubois split from Trotter and the organization.

I believe DuBois realized at some point that violence was not the answer and split from Trotter and the Niagara Movement, however, this did not alter his belief that agitation and protest were the right course. In 1907 he joined with a group of white Republicans to form the National Association For The Advancement of Colored People (NAACP). DuBois was not the leader of the organization, in fact, he never became the leader of the group, rather he was only the editor of their magazine, although he is almost always portrayed as founder and leader of the organization, for obvious reasons.

Henry Moskowitz, Mary White Ovington, William English Walling, Florence Kelley, Oswald Garrison Villard, and Edward Russell, all whites and Republicans, were the actual founders of the NAACP.

False Prophets - Racism Is Not The Problem

If you watch the news, read any news outlet, or follow social media, you are tempted to think racism is everywhere and all the time. It is usually white, anti-black racism that is pointed out. A few years ago, former Attorney General Eric Holder said, "Americans are cowards when it comes to race." In Holders mind, and I wonder if he even believed what he was saying was true, the problem was that we are afraid to see and admit that racism is everywhere. Of course, he, again, was only speaking of white, anti-black racism.

I must admit here I actually agree in part with Mr. Holder's statement. I believe many are cowards when it comes to the issue of race. Where we differ is, I believe Eric Holder is among the biggest cowards and has things reversed. If you will remember, Holder was Attorney General under President Obama. It was while we had a black president and black Attorney General, Holder, that he made these statements. With a black president, attorney general, several cabinet members, and members of Congress we were to believe we were a racist nation.

I really beg to differ with Attorney General Holder. I agree we or many of us are cowards or afraid to speak honestly about race and racism, BUT, from what I see - it is Holder and his band of race baiters that are the problem, the real cowards. In Holder's mind it was a racial crime to speak negatively about Obama or anything he and/or his administration did. From healthcare to foreign policy and regulations, to question any of it had to be only because the President was black. According to Holder, etal, to speak negatively about a black president and his policies was a racist act. His message is we are cowards unless we agree that any criticism of a black president, his actions or policies is racially motivated.

Here is the truth. The true test of a mature, sound, and healthy racial view is when we can criticize a black president, or any other black person, on the merit of their ideas or actions alone, and it NOT be seen as being racially motivated. Let me repeat that a little differently. We will have grown up and arrived on the matter of race when we can criticize or be criticized and one's first thought is not to racism. Maybe our ideas, or maybe we, just suck.

How is it that as a nation we criticized presidents throughout our short history, including Johnson, Nixon, Ford, Carter, Reagan, Bush 1, Clinton, Bush 2, and now Donald Trump and race was considered nowhere in the picture? However, we get a black president and suddenly every criticism is seen as racially motivated. Today, if we see a black or Hispanic member of Congress and criticize their actions or policies, it immediately becomes a racial attack. In fact, if they are merely running for office and a white candidate questions the minority candidate, it is too often considered racially motivated. Who's the real racist and coward here? This has got to stop.

Disallowing criticism of any candidate, their actions or policies creates a system begging for abuse. While not everything President Obama did, the Congressional Black or Hispanic Caucus and others support and do is wrong, every decision, policy and action is also not right. Until we admit that and allow criticism of bad policy and actions, on their merits, we do our nation and our own communities a grave injustice. In fact, if we are honest, one of the reasons, if not the main reason, urban communities languish is that they have been run by black and black supported, so-called leaders, who do not necessarily have our best interests in mind. Their interests are too often about personal power and advantage. Sure, this is not merely a black or urban problem, it is, however, manified more severe in those communities.

Back when I was in college and a "Young radical" myself, so-called "Blaxploitation" films like "Shaft", "Super Fly", "Across 110th Street", "Coffy", and many more correctly portrayed the corruption in inner city communities. I loved those films. I still do. The thing about these films is that much of the corruption was depicted as being at the hands of those community's own politicians and clergy. Politicians and preachers, most often black politicians and preachers, paid off by white criminals and/or politicians, often one in the same, were the ones depicted as the problem in these films. For some reason, however, about the time that Ronald Reagan became president, going forward, the evil politicians, preachers and others were ALWAYS depicted as being white, a southerner, and a Republican. I challenge anyone to show me a film in the last 30-40 years involving a corrupt politician or minister working against this nation, in particularly black and minority communities, where that politician or minister is not white, a southerner and/or a Republican. In many cases they are all four in one. This used to be called brain washing. Today it is considered normal and called "great entertainment" and "speaking truth to power."

Pavlov's Negro

People, particularly black people, have become conditioned. Several years ago, I wrote an article called "Pavlov's Negro." Most people have heard of the Russian Physiologist, Ivan Petrovich Pavlov, and his experiments with animals at the turn of the 20th Century. It has been commonly referred to as "Pavlov's Dog." Dr. Pavlov found that you could condition animals to react to repeated stimuli. Although he did not actually use a bell, but more sophisticated instruments, basically he would use a sound every time the dog was to be fed and measure its reaction to the stimulus of the sound. Eventually the dog would salivate at hearing the mere sound of the bell, associating the sound with food. This led to the correct idea that humans could also be conditioned to respond to certain repeated stimuli. Hitler's propagandist Joseph Goebbels said it this way. "Tell a lie long enough, and strong enough and eventually people will believe you." The lie was usually associated with or after a new benefit or promise of benefit was made. Conversely, after any negative occurrence, blame was put on the opposition. After a while the lies seem plausible and eventually, they become true in the subject's mind.

Let's jump forward about 80 years. In 2005 a group called the National Socialist Movement (NSM), a Neo-Nazi group, announced they were marching through Toledo, Ohio. NSM was marching to protest black gang violence in North Toledo. Upon hearing of this, neighborhood residents, along with the Toledo chapter of the International Socialist Organization, local anarchist organizations, and "anti-racist" groups from outside of Toledo organized a counter protest.

Here is the interesting thing, which brings us back to "Pavlov's Negro", there were less than 10 members of this NSM group. Not a major threat. The anti-protesters, especially the International Socialists, probably a precursor to ANTIFA, and others were over 500 strong. Furthermore, the NSM group never marched but the good citizens of North Toledo never got that word and rioted anyway. Cars and businesses were damaged in the riot. While arrests were made, all were local residents wearing gang colors and NO outsiders were arrested.

When I wrote the article "Pavlov's Negro," I stated that this was too easy. The community had been played. Just as "Pavlov's Dog" reacted to a stimulus even with no food, black folks reacted to the stimulus of cry of "White Supremacy" or "White Nationalists," with no actual or real threat. The mere thought and mention of these terms were enough to set an entire community off. After posting the article on my blog, someone must have read and forwarded it to the leader of the NSM group who had organized the initial march and he responded saying I was exactly right. This was their plan all along, to cause such a reaction.

Adolf Hitler presented the idea of "The Big Lie" in his book "Mein Kampf." Whether it is true or not, it has been attributed later, in a more developed form, to his chief communications officer aka "propagandist," Joseph Goebbels. It goes as follows:

> *"If you tell a lie big enough and keep repeating it, people will eventually come to believe it. The lie can be maintained only for such time as the State can shield the people from the political, economic and/or military consequences of the lie. It thus becomes vitally important for the State to use all of its powers to repress dissent, for the truth is the mortal enemy of the lie, and thus by extension, the truth is the greatest enemy of the State."[1]*

People, we have been and are being played. Lied to about slavery, about political parties, about who is responsible for slavery, and most importantly, what lies behind the sad state of urban communities. The vehicle for the "Big Lie" today, is the major media. They allow Progressive politicians and operators to spread the lie and then, shield the public from the consequences of that lie. The truth is, the policies of the Left and Democrat Party have had and continue to have negative consequences. This is the truth the major media is hiding. The consequences cannot eventually be less painful than those of Nazi Germany.

Chapter 5

WHY US

There are two questions I have asked God for most of my adult life, particularly since I became a Christian believer. One, why have black people been singled out as the world's footstool and two, why have the Jews been persecuted throughout their recorded history?

I am not sure I have a complete answer, however, I think I at least have a clue. It reflects back to the similarities in the Jewish and "Black Experience."

Those who have studied the Old Testament, including the geography, know the walk from Egypt to the land of Cannan should have taken 11 days. Why did this relatively short exodus turn into a 40-year journey? Other than the wrath of God, I believe there are other reasons it took the Jews 40 years. Let me expound in reverse order, beginning with the 4th reason.

Reason 4: **The Crucible.** I believe God put the Jews through the tribulations and trials of wandering to prepare them for what they would experience in retaking the land once they arrived. Time spent in the wilderness hardened then and prepared them to fight and work hard to build a nation. The desert, the heat, the cold, the hunger and thirst, and the battles within and without all played a part in preparing the Jews for becoming a free people in their own land.

Reason 3: **God wanted to reveal that, these were His chosen people** – a people favored by HIM. Beginning with the plagues and the parting of the Red Sea, God showed the Jews, their friends, and their enemies, these are His people, and He is their God.

Let's look at Deuteronomy 9. After wandering around in the desert for 40 years (when they could have arrived in the promised land sooner) and before God allowed them to take possession of the land, He told them why He was driving others out, and why "they" (the Jews) were being given the land.

> *4 "Do not think in your heart, after the Lord your God has cast them out before you, saying, 'Because of my righteousness the Lord has brought me in to possess this land'; but it is because of the wickedness of these nations that the Lord is driving them out from before you. 5 It is not because of your righteousness or the uprightness of your heart that you go in to possess their land, but because of the wickedness of these nations that the Lord your God drives them out from before you, and that He may fulfill the word which the Lord swore to your fathers, to Abraham, Isaac, and Jacob. 6 Therefore understand that the Lord your God is not giving you this good land to possess because of your righteousness, for you are a stiff-necked people."* Deuteronomy 9: 4-6(NKJV)

Ouch!!

Reason 2: **Building a unified and lasting bond among the people.** As shared in the above scripture, the sense of belonging and being responsible for each other sets Jews apart from any other people or group on the planet. Other groups and people have a sense of unity and family, yet there has never been and never will be the sense of belonging we observe among the Jewish population.

We see a similar thing in the military. The tougher the shared circumstances, the closer the men and women are. One of, if not the primary cause of PTSD, is the breaking of that bond. Men and women who eat, sleep, work, fight, love, hate, are injured and die together, have a unique bond which cannot be penetrated or truly understood from without. Only those who had a part in the creation of the bond can possibly know what the bond is like. My father served in the military for 26 years and retired at Ft. Bliss, Texas. Every Saturday my dad would take my mother shopping at the military base PX (Post Exchange) and Commissary. My mother and other wives would shop while my father joined several other Army retirees at a table or tables in the food court. They would sit for hours enjoying one another's company experiencing that common bond. It was and remains a unique bond.

I never served in the military, but I pledged a historically black fraternity. What we 14 young pledges went through bound us to this day. We worked together, suffered harassment and humiliation, but - but to this day each of us holds a special bond. Some of the bonds are stronger than others, yet each of us in that pledge line has and will always have a special relationship.

This explains to some, if not to a great extent, why the "Black Community" is such a tight group when attacked from without. O.J. Simpson, Michael Jackson and many others are an example of individuals who were not necessarily highly thought of in the Black Community, yet once attacked from without, we saw the circle close around them.

I think of the song "Family", by the Canadian group "Mother Mother." I will have to clean up the lyrics in the chorus but I think this truly speaks to the Children of Israel and the descendants of African slaves in America.

Family - by Mother, Mother

They got my blood up in their veins
I get a cut, they feel my pain
They got my heart, they got my soul
They know the stuff nobody knows

When we're out for dinner we're cussing like sailors
The people are staring and talking in whispers
"Hey what's with the strange breed?"

They is my family, they is my family
They might be crazy, but they is my family
You can't get to them unless you get through me
You MESS with them you MESS with me

And when you're standing on the ledge
I'll pull ya down, put you to bed
And if you're bleeding from the heart
I'll come around, and clean it up

When we're at the party we're dancing on tables
And people are staring like they got a peephole
"Hey, look at the strange breed"

They is my family, they is my family
They might be crazy, but they is my family
You can't get to them unless you get through me
You MESS with them you MESS with me

Time in the wilderness hardened and toughened the Jews, as well as instilling a lasting bond visible to this day.

Reason 1: He is the One True God and THEIR God. When the Jews entered the wilderness each nation and tribe had their own god or gods. 400 years in Egypt was 400+ years of Egyptian gods. The Jews had heard of God of Abraham, Isaac and Jacob, yet had not experienced Him. This one God seemed far away, if He existed at all. I believe God's purpose was to introduce himself as the "one and only" God. Through the plagues and the Red Sea experience He was saying: "Hello, please allow Me to introduce myself. 'I Am' that 'I Am,' a God like no other. I have chosen you to reveal Me to the entire world, but first let Me show you."

For 40 years God revealed Himself to the Jewish people and to the world.

He also showed the Jews who they were and forced them to look within, - revealing those things which were good, and those things which must be challenged. In revealing the Jews to the Jews and to the world, God revealed mankind's purpose - with Him and without Him. The Jews and their relationship with God were and remain a picture of God's desired relationship with all of humankind.

34

As with Jews of the past, many people today have forgotten God and are wandering around in the wilderness, searching for their land of promise. He waits and says look at the Jews. What I have done for and with them, I want to do for and with you. Just come to Me and ask. This is God's desire for all communities, Black and other "people of Color" included.

Chapter 6

THE TRUTH ABOUT SLAVERY

H ere, already deep into the 21st Century, it is hard not to daily hear some sort of grievance from some so-called representatives of black Americans regarding the conditions in the "inner city." I do not dispute America's inner cities are in bad shape, but rather than pointing to real issues and solutions, these race doctors want us to take a trip back to the 200 years of slavery as the cause of these issues. They are big on the problems but extremely weak on solutions. It is as though the mere and constant focus on the sad conditions facing urban dwellers is in itself a solution.

In 2019 the New York Times released a magazine insert featuring 10 essays, photos, poems and fictional articles, titled, "The 1619 Project". The stated goal was to challenge the date of the founding of our nation as 1619 and not 1776. As the originator of the project states, the 1619 Project "aims to reframe the country's history by placing the consequences of slavery and the contributions of black Americans at the very center of [the] national narrative." In other words, the Unites States is the nation it is, good and bad, solely as a result of the African slaves and the Trans-Atlantic slave trade.

"The 1619 Project" has been roundly criticized as being inaccurate, but the NY Times and many historians, have declared that in spite of its inaccuracies the importance the work is such that we should overlook these blatant revisionist historical errors.

The "1619 Project" is but one of the many attempts, of late, to re-write the history of our nation.

To me it appears we are supposed to hear about the antebellum era of America and feel sorry for the descendants of slaves. I guess in our supporting the "pity party," it is supposed to somehow miraculously change things, particularly in regard to race and race relations.

Since we have this constant and repeated wallowing in the past injustice of slavery, I think it is important to look at the realities of its origins, historical practice, and its impact upon our nation and worldwide.

If we want to take a hard, honest look at slavery, I must ask you to put aside any pre-notions and what you think you know about the practice of slavery. I ask this because we cannot take a look at the totality of the practice unless we are able to do this. We must particularly lay aside the idea of slavery as a racial issue. I understand this is very hard to do, and I am not saying there is or was not a racial element, particularly as the practice developed through time, but at the core and genesis of the practice, race had and has had little to do with it. It was and is really a matter of class and one group's desire to use another.

As difficult as it may be to do, for the purpose of seeing the bigger picture, we need to look at slavery not as a racial issue but return to the basic societal and economic origins and basis for it, in addition to a spiritual element.

The earliest civilization known to mankind is the Sumerian. The ancient land of Sumer lay in an area which is modern day, southern Iraq. From Sumer, which later became part of the ancient Babylonian Empire, we get the earliest known writings and information on an ancient society and culture. The earliest academically, accepted, recorded information on the practice of slavery is found in the Code of Hammurabi. This is, of course, if you do not believe the Jewish Old Testament record. The code of Hammurabi goes back to the 18th Century B.C. The book of Genesis goes back to the 40th Century B.C. To break that down for its 4000 years before Christ.

Something, which I find extremely interesting, is that the main city of Sumer was the city of Ur. For those who know their bible, Ur is where Abraham was born, where God first spoke to him and where he began his journey. If we accept Abraham's story as found in the book of Genesis, we learn a great deal about the culture. Abraham, by the way, pre-dated Hammurabi by about 200 years.

In Genesis we learn that Abraham had slaves. In fact, Abraham had many slaves. We also learn that at some point various kings raided Sodom, Gomorrah, and two other cities. These kings took the people and property of the kings of Sodom, Gomorrah, two other kings, as well as Abraham's nephew Lot, Lot's family, and Lot's property.

The biblical record states, when Abraham was told this, he gathered **his male servants** and he and his neighbors found, fought the raiding tribes, won back the people and property of the kings of Sodom, Gomorrah, freed Lot, his family, his neighbor's families, and their property, including the slaves.

What I learned from reading this Genesis account and others is that slavery or servitude was a common practice. There were generally two types of servitude back then and later in Europe and Jewish society.

First, was a voluntary servitude based upon economic conditions. It is a harsh but inescapable reality, that while all men and women are created equally, at birth, not all men and women have equal outcomes. In fact, you even see this in families. For whatever the reason, you will have those siblings that succeed and those who do not, or they may all succeed but not all to the same level. For example, three of the most successful and wealthiest men EVER, are Bill Gates, Steve Jobs and Mark Zuckerberg, each of them had siblings. While the names of Bill, Steve and Mark are known worldwide, few, outside of the family and friends know the siblings. Most professional athletes of all stripes have siblings and children. Rarely are those family members equally skilled or successful at whatever the sport.

Why am I making this point? I am making the point that not everyone will achieve the same level of success and/or wealth. It is just a reality. To make the world function, we need people at every level and social status.

Going back to Sumer, (even before and after) while some were very successful and gifted in various trades or endeavors, some were not. The former needed help with certain basic needs, while the latter needed to be fed, clothed, housed and could offer those services to the former. Before the use of money, a barter system was used. I will give you a cow for a certain number of crops. I will give you a number of crops for food if you will build my home, make me some shoes and clothes, etc… This is how basic economics began.

Some individuals and families found it hard to survive on their own and offered to serve the more fortunate. This formed a servant class. In many cases, such as Abraham's household, the servants were treated well and with respect. They were considered near family. In other cases, they were not treated so kindly.

As an example of how it was in Abraham's household look at the story of Eliezer, Abraham's chief servant. He would be like the very trusted head foreman of a giant ranch or thriving manufacturing operation today. He was the most trusted of all of Abraham's family and servants. In fact, in Genesis 15:2 Abraham laments to God that he has no son, no heir and that when he dies, all he has will go to Eliezer. Eliezer was so trusted that when it came time for Abraham's son Isaac to have a wife, Abraham sent Eliezer to find one. He sent the manservant with gifts, livestock, and his full authority to make a deal for a wife for his son. Eliezer was worthy of his trust and he chose wisely in finding Rebecca and negotiating with her family for bride and wife.

When Abraham's wife Sarah could not bear him a child, Sarah offered her servant, Hagar, to be the surrogate mother giving Abraham an heir. This turned out to be a huge mistake but shows the variety and level of relationship between masters and servants.

As with most things in "a fallen world," however, mankind's pride and greed led to manipulation of the system where some, being more shrewd, cunning, and greedy took advantage of the less fortunate. We even saw this is the story of Isaac's son Jacob and his serving his shrewd uncle. Jacob served his uncle for seven years, for the right to marry his uncle's daughter, and then was tricked into serving another seven year term for the wife he initially wanted.

The second condition of servitude was that of those capture as spoils of war. It was normal practice, as seen even in the case of Abraham's encounter with the foreign kings, to make servants and slaves of one's enemies captured in battle.

In post Mosaic Law Israel, Jewish society operated with servants and slaves. Most of these slaves were indentured servants. In that society, a slave or servant was to be offered their freedom after six years of servitude. I say they were offered the freedom because the slave or servant could choose to remain in such a state for life.

There are separate iterations of the treatment of slaves among the nation of Israel, in the Torah (first five books of the Bible). The first in Exodus, then in Leviticus and finally in Deuteronomy.

12 "If your brother, a Hebrew man, or a Hebrew woman, is sold to you and serves you six years, then in the seventh year you shall let him go free from you. 13 And when you send him away free from you, you shall not let him go away empty-handed; 14 you shall supply him liberally from your flock, from your threshing floor, and from your winepress. From what the Lord your God has blessed you with, you shall give to him. 15 You shall remember that you were a slave in the land of Egypt, and the Lord your God redeemed you; therefore, I command you this thing today. 16 And if it happens that he says to you, 'I will not go away from you,' because he loves you and your house, since he prospers with you, 17 then you shall take an awl and thrust it through his ear to the door, and he shall be your servant forever. Also, to your female servant you shall do likewise. 18 It shall not seem hard to you when you send him away free from you; for he has been worth a double hired servant in serving you six years. Then the Lord your God will bless you in all that you do. (Deut. 15:12-18)

The rules for non-Jews was different and essentially unrestricted. The Jews could own non-Jews and their children into perpetuity, which brings me to the second type of slavery, that is the spoils of war.

While the slavery above was voluntary and temporary, or not, there was another type of slavery which was practiced by the Jews. That was captured slaves from the dispossessed lands around them. When they vanquished a city, survivors were made slaves. The treatment of these non-Jewish slaves was very different from that of the fellow Jew.

"And as for your male and female slaves whom you may have— from the nations that are around you, from them you may buy male and female slaves. Moreover, you may buy the children of the strangers who dwell among you, and their families who are with you, which they beget in your land; and they shall become your property. And you may take them as an inheritance for your children after you, to inherit them as a possession; they shall be your permanent slaves." (Lev. 25:44-46)

I would suspect, however, that if a non-Jewish slave converted, the law and treatment reverted to that of a Jew. As Jews were chosen as a witness and type for the relationship God wanted with all mankind, I believe the above situation was one of being with God vs. outside of that relationship.

I have to ask a question here. In the time spent reading the above scripture pertaining to slavery, what color of person did you picture when you read about the Jewish slave and the "Non-Jew?" I think if you are honest, and like me, even writing this, I had to fight the picture of the non-Jew being dark skinned. This shows how conditioned we have become in thinking of slaves as being dark skinned if not black. This has wrought havoc in our modern-day minds and caused the most well-meaning of us to think of an entire race in those terms.

While we think like this, let me make you aware, or remind you that every race on earth has at some point, enslaved others and also been enslaved. Before the Jews became a nation, they were enslaved for several hundred years in Egypt. The Greeks and Romans enslaved people from lands they conquered and were later themselves enslaved. The Scandinavian Vikings raided the coasts of Western Europe and the English Islands taking slaves back with them. The Incas, Mayans, and other indigenous people of the Americas were slaves and were enslaved. The various Asian nations and tribes practiced slavery.

Due to its treacherous climate and other dangers, most of sub-Saharan Africa was off limits to people north of the desert not to mention Europeans. Nevertheless, Bantu tribes had been warring and enslaving one another for eons before the white Europeans arrived.

The Big Lie

I grew up in the 50s and 60s, a time of great upheaval in America regarding race. It was actually a very good time in America, as we woke up, grew up and discovered we are a richer nation as one - not divided. We ended segregation, opened our minds and facilities to everyone and benefited from it. Of course, though, not everything was perfect. As things were changing, some thought it was not changing quickly enough and resorted to various outside influences and sources to deal with their frustration.

I still remember Casius Clay changing his name to Mohammed Ali, followed by Lew Alcindor who changed his name to Kareem Abdul Jabar. This was followed by many black Americans changing their names to Arab names. Much of this was due to the influence of the Black Muslims, now the Nation of Islam and their teaching. Ali would say, "I reject the slave name I was given, for our people's name before we were slaves." This became a fashionable thing to do. I would say that at least Malcolm X did not change his name to either European or Arab rather just a simple X, for the African name he never knew. Maybe he knew something others did not. It sounded like a great idea at the time, considering our history, to take on a great sounding Arab name. There was just one problem with this thinking and Ali's statement, it was a lie. A huge lie that I feel must be exposed.

Historically, on August 8, 1444, just over five years before the birth of Christopher Columbus and 44 years, to the month, before Columbus, an Italian, left Spain for his first historic trip to the "New World," 235 slaves arrived in the port of Lagos, Portugal from the West Coast of Africa. This would mark the beginning of the European slave trade. Over the next 200 years this trafficking in African slaves would turn into the full blown Trans-Atlantic Slave Trade, and the creation of the "Black American" experience. This is what has been taught to black and white children in America from the 3rd or 4th grade on (poorly I might add) and maybe even earlier these days.

Here is what has not been and is still not taught. In fact, as mentioned before, regarding the "1619 Project", we and our children are being led farther and farther from the true history of the African slave trade.

Arab Muslims had been taking slaves from sub-Saharan Africa for over 700 years prior to the first Africans arriving in Europe. May I repeat that?? Seven Hundred years before Europeans took the first slaves out of Africa, Mohammed and his cult of Islam had been taking slaves from sub-Saharan Africa. While the so-called "Middle Passage" or Trans-Atlantic slave routes to the Americas was horrific, the Trans-Saharan slave trade and journey, was much worse. Millions died and/or were mutilated on the journey. All were beaten, starved and brutalized.

43

Males were castrated and women were raped over and over again, unless they were seen as the youngest and best, reserved for the rich and/or powerful Arab, Muslim, Sheikhs, for their Harems.

The enslavement of Africans was and is so ingrained in the conscious of Muslims and Arabs, they never came up with a name for Black people. They just called them Abd, what we would call Abed and translate as "slave." To this day they still do not have a name for the black race. It is still Abd. Some Arab and Muslim apologists will try and tell us they have a word for a black person, which would be a translation of the color black, but that is not the word they use for a black person. So, when you hear any ignorant black or any other person speak of the evils of the "Middle Passage" and then support Islam and/or the Arab world, ask them to show you how the Arab slave trade was shorter and better than the Trans-Atlantic trade.

We will take a good look at The Nation Of Islam also known as Black Muslims later, but let me say here that they have made a huge deal about Christian slave traders and holders. To this day many in the Nation of Islam and black supremacists call Christianity the White Man's religion. This was a blight on the Christian faith, and many under the guise of religion perverted it to their own personal gain. I am merely wanting to show here that to single out Christianity as the sole practitioners of slavery and the slave trade is a grave mistake. We have seen people of all faiths abusing and misusing this, but it was Christians who preached, worked, fought, and died to set slaves free and end the practice. Christians continue to lead the fight against modern day slavery, be it in the nations still practicing the trade of African slaves or sex trafficking.

It was Christians, who were abolitionists, not Muslims. Wilberforce his allies in England, the Quakers, the Wesley brothers and many of our founding fathers in America were. In fact, while the Trans-Atlantic Slave trade to the U.S. ended, by law, in 1807 and slavery within the nation officially ended in the U.S. in 1863, it continued in Arab lands, under Muslim rule well into the 20th Century. A black market of African slaves even continues today, but we hear little of this.

As this book is written for Americans and western readers, let's take a closer look at the Trans-Atlantic trade and slavery in the United States of America, specifically, which for some reason we are told was the most brutal and barbaric form of slavery. Even though, as I pointed out earlier, the Trans-Saharan trade was far worse, far more barbaric, pre-dated and post-dated the Trans-Atlantic trade, especially to the British colonies.

What most Americans are taught and know about American slavery from primary school, is that the first black slaves brought to America arrived in Virginia, in 1619. The "1619 Project" makes much, too much, of that event. There is, however, evidence there may have been more Africans, free and enslaved, brought to the Americas prior to 1619. This is most likely true, if we remember that there were territories outside of the 13 British colonies, under Spanish, French, Dutch and Portuguese rule. But keeping with mainstream history, and as colonial slavery in the 13 colonies is what is used to bludgeon white Americans or Americans of European birth, we will use the 1619 date as the beginning of the Trans-Atlantic African slave trade.

What we have not been taught, and what I am sure you may be shocked to learn, is those initial 20 or so "slaves" were not actually slaves. Believe it or not, as an institution, slavery was not a legal practice in the Virginia colony in 1619. Indentured servitude, however, was a legal practice. Indentured servitude held black and white servants alike for a pre-set period of time after which the servant was free from servitude. This was the case in Virginia until 1655.

Now this is where things get really interesting and I would have to say throws a huge wrench into the whole thinking and teaching on slavery in America. That is the story of John Casor, and how he became the first permanent slave in the 13 colonies.

We learned in grade school, the first African slaves to the 13 Colonies arrived at Jamestown in 1619. What we were not told, however, is that these were not actually slaves. They were indentured servants, just as those from Europe. The 1619 group was initially intended to be slaves, headed to Vera Cruz, Mexico on a Portuguese ship. The ship, however, was attacked by pirates and a portion of the stock of slaves was then brought to Virginia. As slavery was illegal in Virginia, I repeat, SLAVERY WAS ILLEGAL IN VIRGINIA, the shipment was sold as indentured servants.

One of those original indentured servants was named "Antonio." Antonio was from Angola and had been captured initially by Arab slave traders and sold to a European Trans-Atlantic merchant of slaves to the Americas. He happened to be on the ship headed to Vera Cruz, where he would have been a slave. He was instead brought to Virginia as one of the original African indentured "servants." Antonio served his term of indenture on a Virginia farm where he met his wife. When his term of indenture ended, he was set free, was granted his own land by the Virginia colony, changed his name to Anthony Johnson and started his own tobacco farm. He was very successful and was then entitled to purchase his own indentured servants. At the time, lifetime servitude or slavery was not allowed, by law, in any of the 13 colonies. Anthony Johnson, purchased the indenture of five servants, four white and one black. The black servant was named John Casor. When Casor served his time of indenture, he went to a white neighboring farmer named Robert Parker, told him he had served his term under Johnson and offered to work for him. He signed a new indenture contract with Parker. Anthony Johnson said Casor had not fulfilled his term of indenture, took Robert Parker to court and sued him to get his property (Casor) back. The original court found in favor of Robert Parker but on appeal, the appellate court found in favor of Johnson.

It turned into a nightmare for Parker, Casor and generations of Africans in America and their descendants. Parker was ordered to pay all court costs, and Casor was ordered to return to the Johnson farm, to work there for the rest of his life. This was the first case in which a person who had committed no crime was sentenced to lifetime servitude in the 13 Colonies. There had been another case about 12 years prior when another black indentured servant John Punch ran away in violation of his indenture contract, but that was seen as a crime and a different circumstance. The Johnson/Casor affair led to the sentencing of a person into a lifetime of slavery for no crime. Despite other neighboring farmers testifying that John Casor had indeed served his time, this court never the less sentenced him to a life of slavery.

It is pretty clear that this case was one the plantation and farm owners wanted and they found the right court to rule in their favor. They had wanted to change the indenture laws and this case gave them the perfect opportunity to do so.

While it was a white court, that found in favor of the slave owner, is it not ironic the case which sentenced a black person to slavery, and opened the door to a future where an entire race could be enslaved without just cause, would be at the behest of another black man. Just as it was Africans selling other Africans into slavery, even in this country, it was a black man that set the stage for over two hundred years of the practice in this land of ours.

The Vision of Our Founders

Much is made about Thomas Jefferson and George Washington, without a doubt the two most important figures in the founding of our nation, being slave owners. That known fact is true. What is not spoken of however, are the facts behind their slave holdings and the institution inherited by these men, as it was by everyone living at that time. What set these men apart was the fact that they initiated the end of slavery in America. As mentioned before, the institution of lifetime servitude began in about 1653 with the case of John Casor.

While the Declaration of Independence and the Constitution did not abolish slavery when signed, it began the ticking clock. From the beginning Jefferson inserted a ticking time bomb into the Declaration when he wrote, "We hold these truths to be self-evident that ALL men are created equal, and endowed by their creator with certain unalienable rights, of LIFE, LIBERTY and THE PURSUIT OF HAPPINESS." In order to get the southern slaveholding states to join in the revolution against the Crown, they were forced to not push for the abolition of slavery at that moment. By inserting that line into the Declaration of Independence in 1776, they knew, at some point, in the not too distant future, a future legislature would have to wrestle with that question and particularly the phrase, "ALL MEN." Furthermore, when the Constitution was finally ratified in June of 1788 it contained the 3/5th Clause.

Three Fifths Clause

The "Three Fifths Clause of the Constitution is one of the most misunderstood and misinterpreted pieces of work ever. I believe it is most often misrepresented, purposefully, to deceive and undermine our founding. The founders were not able to achieve the abolition of slavery at the signing of the Declaration in 1776. Never the less, several of the state legislatures and legislators, particularly in the northern states continued to fight for an end to slavery, from the beginning. At the time of the adoption of the Articles of Confederation and the Constitution, several things converged at the same time. One of these was the apportionment of representatives to the House of Representatives and how this was to be done. As most of us know, or should know, seats in the House of Representatives are apportioned according to the population of a state. As a side note, it is very interesting that today over 200 years later we are still fighting over whom we should count for these census figures, with Democrats on one side and Republicans on the other. As we have recently seen in this fight it is the same now as it was back then. While Southern Democrats were not willing to count their slaves as persons with the rights of citizenship, they did want to count them for the purpose of population in order to get more seats in the House. What this would have done is give them a perpetual majority in the Legislature. Northern legislators said this was not fair or right and decided, if this were to be the case, they should be able to count their livestock for the census. The north had many more cows, pigs, and other animals they could use for the census. In other words, IF southerners wanted to say their slaves were not people, and livestock, but wanted to count them as such for political reasons, and apportionment, the northern free states should have the right to count their non-human "livestock" for the same. Eventually a compromise was reached and it was agreed that for the purpose of the census, for **APPORTIONMENT OF HOUSE SEATS,** slaves would count only as 3/5th of a person.

For someone to say black people were counted as 3/5th human is just plain wrong. If that were the case you could say Democrats counted them as ZERO. The 3/5th apportionment actually worked toward slowing down the spread of slavery in the new territories, although it did not succeed in abolishing the practice altogether. Had it not been included in the Articles of the Constitution, I believe, emancipation would have been delayed even longer.

After the 3/5th Clause, below are several anti-slavery bills that were passed and the presidents who signed the legislation.

Anti - Slavery Legislation From The Beginning

1787 - Northwest Ordinance – George Washington: This was one of the first anti-slavery acts which actually predated the US constitution. It was initially passed by the Confederation Congress in 1785 and later ratified by the 1st US Congress in 1787 and reaffirmed by Congress in 1789. Article 6 of the NW Ordinance outlawed slavery in the territories north and west of the Ohio River.

1794 - Federal Slave Trade Act - George Washington: Criminalized the importing or exporting of slaves to or from the US by any US person, company, or vessel.

1800 - Slave Trade Act - John Adams: Enacted to strengthen and build upon the Slave Trade Act of 1794, forbidding the importation of slaves to the US. Banned ownership of companies and vessels involved in the slave trade and added that no US citizen could legally work aboard a slave ship.

1807 - The Act Prohibiting Importation of Slaves - Thomas Jefferson: Banned the importation of slaves to the US from any nation and on any vessel

1820 - An act to protect the commerce of the United States and punish the crime of piracy - James Monroe: This was an anti-piracy act but it was amended to make slave trading **a capital crime**.

1820 - Missouri Compromise - James Monroe: This bill agreed that for every slave state there would be an equal free state.

In spite of these attempts to end slavery Southern Democrats continued to fight abolition, created new laws and rules, and with the help of the courts, were able to not only stop abolition from spreading, but had the practice of slavery threatening to expand. The Dred Scott decision, in 1857, was the final straw that finally set the wheels of emancipation into motion. The Dred Scott decision essentially said that the rights and privileges of freedom enjoyed by others did not apply to and could NEVER be conferred onto a black person. The Supreme Court held that the rights of citizenship conferred by the US Constitution were not intended for the black people, therefore, black men and women, slave OR free, could never be considered citizens.

Members of the Whig Party and Northern Democrats who became disgusted with their party's refusal to end slavery, and their working for its expansion, saw the situation was not going to change under the current system. In 1854 these two entities united and formed the Republican Party. Please understand and do not be deceived by any revisionist history, the Republican Party was formed for one purpose and one purpose alone. To END SLAVERY! They set forth their first candidates in 1856 but lost. Four years later, in 1860 the now six-year-old, Republican Party won the presidency of the United States with their candidate Abraham Lincoln. Two years later the Emancipation Proclamation was signed by Abraham Lincoln and slavery in the United States of America officially ended by executive order. In order to solidify this, however, the Thirteenth Amendment was ratified by the Congress, in December of 1865, abolishing slavery finally and officially.

The 13th and 14th Amendments were ratified and became law granting freedom and all the rights of citizenship upon the Black race, former slave and free. This, however, was not the end of slavery or the Trans-Atlantic Slave trade. The "Middle Passage" slave route continued to Central and South America late into the 1800s. Brazil being the last country to end the trade, under British pressure in 1850, finally ending their practice of slavery in 1888.

As noted above slavery and especially the slave trade in South America, continued well beyond that of North America. As bad as this may be, and it was very bad, it is still a drop in the bucket when compared to the over 1000-year slave trading history of Arab, Muslims. When we look at (1500 to 1800) three hundred years of the Atlantic Slave Trade, it is but a third of the Arab slave trade.

I want to drive home the point that we have been lied to, hidden from the facts, and misled into thinking the United States was and is the worst enemy of the African and their descendants. We have black people adopting African and Arab names, wanting to sound hip by learning Swahili, wearing African and Arab garb while cursing the United States of America for its past. Little do they know or do they want it known that Swahili was developed as a language for and from the East African, Arab slave trade. Swahili was specifically, a slave language.

The Truth About The Middle Passage

Another little known or published fact is that of the 11 to 13 million African slaves transported to the Americas, only about 5% actually came to the colonies. Ninety five percent ended up in central and South America. Brazil was the major importer of slaves to the Americas, which was natural, being a Portuguese colony, with the Portuguese having been the original European slave traders.[1]

The 5% that were brought to the colonies eventually grew to become 17% of the population, at their peak and an integral part of the fiber of this nation. Black men and women, the descendants of slaves, through their inventions and hard work, have made major contributions in agriculture, science, medicine, the arts, sports, and of course the law and politics of this nation.

We should not need a "Black History Month," as in every month, if not every week, we can find a descendant or descendants of African slaves that have made major contributions to this great nation of ours. We cheapen our contribution and impact by being relegated to a month out of the year. The descendants of African slaves, both men and women, have given so much throughout the calendar year that it hurts me to have us make so much out of one month. We have been made to believe this month makes us special. What a lie we have been fed. We are now special, like Hispanic American Month, Gay Pride Month, Asian American and Pacific Islander Heritage Month, and yes, National

Pet Month. We are so much more than that, but have accepted scraps thrown to us as appeasement, to keep us quiet and in our place.

Too Close To See

Maybe it is hard to get a proper view of who we are and what power we have from within the framework of our country. Maybe we need to see it from outside. I have travelled the world over and no matter where I have gone; my citizenship in the United States of America has been respected. Europe, Africa, Australia, New Zealand, and even in South Africa during Apartheid, I was respected and protected because I was an American.

In 1984, while in South Africa, I ran into situations where my U.S. citizenship was like a magical cloak. I had people come at me to treat me like a lowly cowering subject until I spoke or showed my passport. Once that happened, it was they who cowered, literally and apologetically. NO other nation on earth gives its citizens as much natural power and authority as the United States of America. We, descendants of African slaves, have inherited that power and authority. It is time we lived and acted like it.

If we look around the world today and look at the status of black people, particularly the descendants of slaves, no place on this earth are we treated better or have we achieved more than in this nation, The United States of America. What nation has more black millionaires, CEOs, military officers, members of the national legislature, and so many other noble and notable positions of status and power? No nation or continent, Africa, Asia, Europe, Central or South America, or Australia has been a greater home to and done more, for and with its black inhabitants than these United States of America. It truly is and has been "the land of opportunity."

What about Reparations?

For the past several years we have seen an ever-growing demand for Slave Reparations. The supposed plaintiff in this reparations case are the descendants of African slaves in America. There are two grounds given for the payment of reparations to the "Class." 1) Many of the largest and richest corporations in America became so on the backs of slave labor. 2) The dehumanization and injury suffered by slaves during and in the aftermath of slavery, has had a lasting and soul damaging affect upon the descendants of slaves caused the poverty and ills affecting predominantly black neighborhoods across America.

While it is true that some of the successful companies in this nation benefited from slavery, to say it was solely or largely because of this is misguided. It also shows a poor understanding of business. Several of the companies listed as "guilty corporations" were not around during this time and are only listed because they purchased or took over holdings from companies that had been involved in the trade or practice. Those purchased companies most likely failed because theirs was a poor business model, and if slavery was the only thing which made them successful, their success ended with slavery. If slavery was the secret to their success, how could they remain successful after the end of the practice? In addition, most, if not all of these corporations and even universities, have also since, offered good jobs and careers, as well as a top-notch education, to black students. In addition, many of these companies and schools now have black board members, educators and executives.

In regard to the lasting, debilitating effect of slavery upon the black psyche, that is just a very poor excuse for failure. If the dehumanizing brutalization and constant attack upon a race of people were capable of that, there would be NO successful Jews in the world. Purges, Pogroms, discrimination and even genocide, have been suffered by Jews throughout history, from every other race and culture. They have had their personal property, their land and their lives taken throughout history, yet there appears to be no lasting psychological effect upon them. How is that? I will touch upon that later, but we see Jews not only survive but thrive after every attempt to extinguish their very existence.

As to the second and even more complicated aspect, reparations, who is entitled to them and how much are they entitled to? Let's take the Obama family for example. Barack's father's people (Africans) sold us into slavery and his mother's people bought us. Does he get any reparations or should he actually pay them? Then we have his wife and children. Does Michelle's background count more than Barack's entitling her and/or she and the children to get a full share? The Obama's are just the tip of the iceberg.

What about the case of Anthony Johnson and John Casor, the first totally innocent person, legally condemned to slavery for life? As told before, Johnson was black, and a former indentured servant himself, who after his service bought and enslaved John Casor and his family, for the rest of their lives in a court case that set the course of slavery in America for the next 200 years. Do Casor's descendants receive reparations from Johnson's? Do Johnson's descendants collect because they are black or do they pay?

Then we have the very interesting and tricky situation of American Indians aka "Native Americans." A great deal has been said about the "Five Civilized Tribes," Cherokee, Chickasaw, Choctaw, Creek (Muskogee), the Seminole and the "Trail of Tears." This refers to the forceful uprooting of the tribes from their ancestral homes in the old south, westward to Oklahoma between 1830 and 1850. This is portrayed as one of the saddest events in American history. It was not the easiest trip for the displaced "natives," as they dealt with near starvation, and the elements on the journey.

What we do not hear about, however, is the fact that those same tribes, who sided with the Confederacy, during the civil War, owned African slaves who travelled with them on the trail.

Several years ago, I was hosting a talk radio show and decided to do a show on the descendants of the "Freedmen." For those who do not know, the "Freedmen" are black members or former members of the "Five Civilized Tribes." These were originally the slaves of those same tribes. As I was interviewing this lady regarding the attempt by one of the tribes to purge their black members, I mentioned the trail of tears and how awful it was on those Indians. She kind of scoffed and said, "who do you think was carrying those Indians' bags on that journey?" I almost fell out of my seat. I learned that during the Civil War, those tribes had decided to join with the Confederate States against the Union. After the war ended and the treaties were signed with the Confederate states, a separate treaty was signed between the US and the Tribes. As a part of that treaty the Tribes had two choices. 1) Give their freed slaves 40 acres and a mule, or 2) make them full members of the tribe. While some of the tribes chose to do the former, several decided to make the "Freedmen" members of their tribe. This held until they tried to purge the "Freedmen" from their rolls and deny them tribal rights and privileges.

This brings me to the question, do the tribes still owe something in reparations to their former slaves? If so what? If not, why? Do the descendants of the former slaves of the Tribes qualify for slavery reparations from the U.S.?

As the majority of black Americans have some mixture of white, American Indian blood or both in them, how do we measure the amount of reparations they should receive OR pay? And again, who do the descendants of John Casor get reparations from?

We also have other, even stickier questions. What about Arab countries? Do they owe reparations? If not why? If the United States owes reparations for 200 years of chattel slavery what do the Arabs owe for 1200 years of it? And what about the European nations, Portugal, Spain, Holland and England that traded in slaves across the Atlantic?

Chapter 7

CHRISTIANS WERE NOT ALWAYS NOR THE ONLY SLAVE OWNERS

I n all the talk of slavery as an institution at the hands of white Christians, we seem to have ignored the treatment of white Christians throughout the ages. I question whether the slave traders often portrayed as Christian, were true believers in Christ and His gospel. For the sake of this segment, however, let's assume they were "followers of Christ." The period of white, so-called Christians trafficking and trading African slaves is short in comparison to white Christians being enslaved and abused. I have stated earlier that all nations and people groups have been enslaved and have enslaved others, but in America in particular, we have heard for decades from Black antagonists that Christianity is a "White Man's" religion - a religion used to enslave Black people.

This is mostly from a lack of historical knowledge and understanding. Children in American and western European schools are taught that White's and white Christians in particular, were the evil originators and perpetuators of the slave trade. Unfortunately, after years of this indoctrination even an ever-growing number of White's believe this. It is a very sad state when an entire race accepts fiction for fact, when it portrays them negatively. This has led to the mental pandemic called "White Guilt." We have already discussed the fact that slavery is almost as old as mankind itself. We have also discussed the fact that Islam, under Mohammed, initiated the brutal Trans-Saharan slave trade. What we have not covered though, is the enslavement of and brutality toward Whites and Christians themselves.

There have been books and writings on the mistreatment and enslavement of Christians and there was a time when films were made about this. Yet, for the past 60 years or so we have not seen this story told. I remember as a young child my Black father and so many of his generation being moved and inspired by stories and historical films like "The Robe", "Demetrius", "Ben-Hur" and others (made by Jewish filmmakers). My father would take me to see these films to learn how Christians were persecuted. Color was not considered.

Today there are forces at work, which will not only not cover these themes, but which are rewriting them. Seldom, if ever is the persecution of White Christians taught or depicted. Millions of Christians have been persecuted and murdered in the most brutal of ways, throughout history, including modern history. From Islamic lands to Communist Eastern Europe, Christians have been, and in many countries continue to be tortured, mistreated, and enslaved. From the time of the founding of the Church of Jesus Christ, His disciples suffered persecution. First at the hands of the Jewish rulers and then by the Romans and Roman Empire. They were beaten, starved, crucified, burned at the stake, fed to wild animals, and made to fight in arenas for sport. They were enslaved in Rome and throughout Europe, from the first century through the Roman Empire's domination, and thereafter by those who conquered the Romans in central and northern Europe. From the 5th to the 11th century, Vikings from Norway, Sweden, and Denmark, raided the coasts of England, Ireland, and from Holland all the way to Spain, capturing slaves from Ireland and England as well as the west coast of Europe. Entire Coastal towns disappeared as a result of the occupants being carried away and enslaved, with those left fleeing from the coasts.

Then there was the treatment of Christians in the former Communist block of Eastern Europe. Among these one, if not the most brutal, was the tiny nation of Albania. Under Communist rule beginning in 1946, an extremely brutal attempt was made to rid the nation of Christianity. The 2003 film, "*I am David*" tried to depict a small aspect of this period, though the reality was much worse. In the prison camps, the slow torture took many forms. Jan Gardin, a Jesuit survivor, recorded in his journal:

"Most of them were beaten on their bare feet with wooden clubs; the fleshy part of the legs and buttocks were cut open, rock salt inserted beneath the skin, and then sewn up again; their feet, placed in boiling water until the flesh fell off, were then rubbed with salt; their Achilles tendons were pierced with hot wires. Some were hung by their arms for three days without food; put in ice and icy water until nearly frozen; had electrical wires placed in their ears, nose, mouth, genitals, and anus; burning pine needles placed under fingernails; forced to eat a kilo of salt

and having water withheld for 24 hours; boiled eggs put in their armpits; teeth pulled without anesthetic; tied behind vans and dragged; left in solitary confinement without food or water until almost dead; forced to drink their own urine and eat their own excrement; put in pits of excrement up to their necks; put on a bed of nails and covered with heavy material; put in nail-studded cages which were then rotated rapidly."[1]

Then there was Japan as depicted in the 2016 Martin Scorsese film, "Silence." This is the story of Catholic priests attempting to evangelize Japan and the torture and killing of them and their Japanese converts. I share these few examples to say slavery and inhumanity is not limited to racial motives. It is about man's inhumanity to man.

This inhumanity continues as we wrestle with racial issues. In America, they are paled by comparison against what is going on elsewhere. I have spoken elsewhere of the Muslim slave trade where millions of sub-Saharans (Black Africans) were taken across the Sahara Desert to be abused and enslaved in Arab lands, from the 8th century and the time of Mohammed. I have not yet spoken of the Muslim enslavement of White Europeans and Christians, or the fact it continues today.

From the 16th to the 19th century, North African pirates, known as the Barbary Pirates raided ships and coastal areas from Italy in the Mediterranean, to the western coast of England and Ireland. Because the Barbary Coast covered most of North Africa, they easily captured over 1 million European slaves. Many who were willing to convert to Islam were freed, while those who would not spent their entire lives as slaves.

Thomas Jefferson sent the still young US Marines to join the Swedish navy to invade North Africa and secure the release of US and other captives in the 1st Barbary War, ending in 1805. The pirate raids started up again and because the US was busy with the War of 1812, the Barbary Pirates were free to plunder once more, for a period.

In 1815 raids and piracy against US ships resumed one more time. President James Madison sent an even stronger US Naval force with the help of a Dutch naval force to end it. Although no more US ships were attacked and captured, the pirates continued to raid the southern European nations along the Mediterranean coast until the French captured Algiers in 1930 and brought order to the southern coast of the Mediterranean Sea.

Believe it or not, to this day slave markets continue to trade in African countries, yet we are told very little. In May of 2017, the website face2faceafrica reported:

> *"South Africa is one of the many African countries that suffered immensely during the Trans-Atlantic Slave Trade. Unfortunately, things haven't changed much in terms of ending slavery in this rainbow nation: Last year, (2016) the Global Slavery Index estimated that close to 250,000 modern slaves exist in South Africa today. About 103,461 victims of this practice were identified to have been subjected to commercial sexual exploitation. It has also been widely alleged that the majority of wine production companies in South Africa still practice slavery. Among the most common forms of slavery in SA include forced labor, human trafficking, debt bondage, child exploitation, and forced marriage."*

In relation to the constant clamor over past slavery in America, in 2017 CNN covered today's slave trade and even showed slave markets in Libya. This was but one of the many places where Africans are trafficked and traded to this day. Mauritania, an Islamic state, on the northwest coast of Africa, is the last country to officially abolish slavery.

They did so in 1981 but then did not criminalize it until 2007. Even so, there are believed to be some 90,000 persons still held in slavery in that nation to this day. Mauritania is not the only nation that continues to buy and sell people. I present this information to hopefully get our attention off of the silly, relatively minor inconveniences we, as Black people, suffer here in America today and look to the truly serious issues our black brethren are suffering worldwide. It gets back to Joseph and "What you meant for evil, God meant for good, THAT HE MIGHT SAVE MANY LIVES." *Genesis 50:20.* Are we working to save the lives of our brethren in Africa or are we too busy focusing on our problems here?

Chapter 8
RACE AND RACISM

I have stated there is no such thing as racism. I can just see heads exploding at the thought, particularly at this time when race and racism seem to be at the forefront of everyone's mind. We constantly hear the terms institutional racism, systemic racism, racial injustice, racial privilege, and critical race theory. So, how can I dare to say there is NO SUCH THING as racism. I can state that because it is true. Let me try and avoid any misunderstanding.

While I said there is no such thing as race or racism, I did not say there is no injustice based on skin color, ethnicity, sex, national origin, or social status. What I said was "there is no such thing as racism". What I mean is, we confuse racism with something else. That something else is prejudice. Prejudice is not limited to race or pigmentation. For example, I can be prejudiced against someone simply because they vote for a different party, belong to a different religion, root for, or wear the colors of a different team. Racism is simply an expression of the sins lust, envy, and pride. In fact, you could call prejudice "Pride-judice". In Northern Ireland there are Protestants and Catholics, in the middle east it is Jews, Muslims, and Christians, and in Africa and South America it has been tribe against tribe since the beginning of time. In India, the Hindus are against the Buddhists, and worldwide there are others. Name the country and I can identify prejudice within each.

In America we are currently seeing the most extreme division our country has experienced in over 150 years. A division based on the idea of race and racism. Despite the immense strides minorities have made in 150 plus years, a segment of our society is clamoring for and demanding more. I am not only disheartened by a national movement toward this thinking but alarmed by the fact so many supposedly, men and women of faith have bought into the idea of racism as the thing holding "people of color" back. I think of George W. Bush's statement the "soft bigotry of low expectations". This is, in fact, a major cop out and undercuts the faith these men and women are supposed to represent.

These people should know better and teach better. To buy into this way of thinking is denying the faith black and white pastors preach. They are saying prejudice and man's injustice is greater than God and His plan for us.

I was born in a small German village six years after the end of World War II. The US military was segregated and the powers that be decided to poke the Nazi, Germans in the eye by putting all black battalions in former Hitler strongholds. My village was a suburb of Nuremberg where the "War Trials" were held. When I was born my parents were not married, and my mother lived in a 15 by 20 foot room, in a multi-roomed shack that housed ten families. The Germans called them "The Barracks." It was what (I guess) you might call a German version of "The Projects." There were five units on one side of a hallway separating the two five-unit sides. Each family lived in one of the small rooms. The walls were made of a single sheet of plywood separating each room from the next - the external walls were the same except they had a window. Each room had one coal burning, "Pot Belly" stove for heating and cooking. These conditions were a result of losing the war and living in a country with no money because the leader spent it all on the war.

One thing you will always find among the poor though, is children and there were lots of children living in these places. My very first girlfriend of sorts, Hildegard, was there. Actually, she was more of a best friend at the time. I was born in the home of a friend of my mother, was a few weeks old when I moved to "The Barracks" with my mother. I was five years old when we left. As poor as we kids were, we had a wonderful time. I did not know I was black nor did I know the others were white and vice versa. We also had no concept that we were poor. We just were, and we had fun. Man! Did we have fun!

I was the only "Brown Baby" in the pack, yet I was the leader of the pack. Our little barracks was near the road to Nuremberg, the one US military troops would travel on their way to and from maneuvers. How we knew they were coming I have no idea but the "slum rat network" got the word out. We would run up an embankment to the highway, stand and yell at the troops for candy. Somehow, we knew Americans had chocolate and gum. As was always the case too, the generosity of

American troops was on display. They would throw Hershey bars and Wrigley's chewing gum as they rode past in their military vehicles. Seeing me, a mixed-race child, they knew I had an American father so I was targeted and always got the lion's share of the candy. I still remember returning home with my candy and showing it to my mother. I remember one incident where my mother asked if she could have a bite of my candy bar and I told her no. She was so mean and cruel that she proceeded to open and eat the entire candy bar in front of me. I am still traumatized.

Think about it, here I was a lone black kid, "a fly in the milk" you could say, but I was king of the hill. The all white kids and their all white parents treated me with love and care. Some of the fathers were former German soldiers and had just a few years earlier fought a war against my father's military. Some of the women had lost fathers, brothers and husbands to my father's army. Yet there was no bitterness, no racism or prejudice. Why, because we were all poor and in this together. They did not have time to think about prejudice. The ten families occupying this expanded shack formed a bond of common respect and care for one another. The men and women married or single worked hard to get back what they had lost, and they did. They never treated my mother, who had a child out of wedlock and a black child at that, poorly.

I attended an all-white Catholic pre-school where I was exalted above my classmates. I could walk into any shop in that town at the age of 3 or 4 (a child could do that without fear back then) and they would ask what I wanted and give it to me with the magic words, "My Oma (grandma) will pay for it".

I am not saying this just to tell you my story. I am telling you to say, racism is too often used as a crutch, a get out of jail free card, and an exploited term for the benefit of some seeking their own personal gain, and others who feel the need to have a grievance. The more we focus on it, the more it grows in our minds and the more deadly it becomes.

Things are out of control people and we need to get it back under. Should we fail to gain control of this monster, I am afraid Booker T. Washington's warning will come to pass. We are at that point in our nation's history. Speaking of the descendants of African slaves, Dr. Washington said:

"We shall constitute one third and more of the ignorance and crime of the South, or one third its intelligence and progress; we shall contribute one third to the business and industrial prosperity of the South, or we shall prove a veritable body of death, stagnating, depressing, retarding every effort to advance the body politic."[1]

The we, he spoke of, was descendants of African slaves. He spoke of this in terms of "The South", but it applies today to the entire nation.

I am asking you today, to eliminate the words race and racism from your vocabulary. Think of us, as a nation, like my "slum rat posse". See us all as one. Some with dark hair, some blond and some red, some tall, and some short. Some with brown eyes, blue eyes, green eyes; just the differences God created. Different pigmentation, red, yellow, black, and white.

Do not like or dislike me for my pigmentation or lack thereof, do not respecter disrespect me for my social status, or the type of work I do. Like me or do not like me because of my actions not my immutable characteristics. As Jesus said, unless we become like children, we shall not enter the Kingdom of Heaven. Let us become like that small horde of little German "slum rats," my little "Feucht Posse", who had no fear, and no understanding of who or what we were or what others thought of us. We simply did not care, we were happy, we were one.

Chapter 9

FROM THE PLANTATION TO THE KENNEL
(From Slaves to Pets)

F or years, many black Conservatives have used "The Plantation" analogy to describe the relationship of black Americans to the Democrat Party and their Liberal-Progressive leaders. The idea is that most black Americans have been re-enslaved by Liberal ideology and groups to do their bidding. The Democrat or Liberal Plantation is considered by black Conservatives as the new space occupied by Liberal black American, ideological slaves. A space run by their white Liberal masters and black overseers - the new plantation

While I think this fits in many cases, I have recently come to see a different analogy – the comparison to a kennel. It appears to me masses of Black People have become "The Pets" of the Liberal Progressive movement and the Democrat Party, and now live in a virtual kennel.

Here is my reasoning. The plantation was a very harsh place, where African slaves and their offspring were worked and abused. They were chained, beaten, had NO social, cultural, or political freedom, and saw their families torn apart at the whim of their owners. If they did not work hard enough or "misbehaved," harsh and abusive measures were taken. To keep them in line they were beaten, starved and the women raped. They were not free to attend school or be otherwise educated, to take part in the political process, or participate in society at large.

We do not see that today. Black Americans are free to learn, socialize, earn an income, and participate in the political process without being beaten, physically abused or otherwise oppressed, except by one another or the white Democrat masters, when we forget our place.

Black people are by and large not treated harshly as a matter of routine. Today a great deal are treated as special, and often pampered pets, regardless of what "Black Lives Matter," Colin Kaepernick, LeBron James, and a kennel full of athletes, entertainers, politicians and the other "Pampered Pets" might try to make us believe. For the most part they are no longer beaten, abused, or forced to work for "The Man".

In truth millions of Black American, "Inner City," "Ghetto dwellers," are fed, housed, and clothed for NOT working. Meanwhile, many outside "the Hood," make a good living merely doing **"the man's" bidding and toeing the Party line.** Many others are pampered and fawned over, especially the obedient, well groomed, trained, and behaved athletes, entertainers, loyal Democrats and "left" leaning, politicians. They are given lots of freedom, special treatment, and treats, but when their masters call them to "Heel," they know their place, come running and obey.

My elderly mother has a pet, a French Poodle. It would try and run off if you left the door open. We had to keep it on a leash if we took it outside so we would not have to go find it. One day I decided I wanted to try and train the dog. I would take the dog out on a leash and carry dog treats. It was a leash that was spring loaded and could be let out about 30 to 40 feet. When the dog stayed with me or would come when I called, I would let the leash out and it would get a treat. Eventually the dog stayed in close proximity and came when I called. It would go 30 or 40 feet and had the freedom to walk around without a leash. When I called, it came. It has ever since obeyed my commands and stayed nearby. The dog is no longer on a physical leash but on a mental one, knowing if it is obedient it will not be beaten, it will be well treated and possibly given a treat. This is how I see the relationship of Black Americans to the Liberal Progressive movement and the Democrat Party. They think they are free but in reality, they stick close, looking for and waiting for that treat.

If this were not enough, many of these pampered pets have been trained as attack dogs. They have been trained to attack anyone their masters ask them to attack. **"See Republicans, sic 'em boy, sic 'em girl. See Conservatives, black, white, or other, sic 'em."** Oh.... and if one of the pets get the idea that they might want to be free, the obedient "pets" attack and force them back into submission.

In 2000 the Republicans were accused of stealing the Bush v. Gore election. We were led to believe voters in Florida's black neighborhoods were intimidated by the GOP and "Black Votes" were improperly counted due to "hanging chads". I was having lunch with a black Democrat about a year after this and told him I was a Republican. He looked around to ensure no one was listening and whispered, "I have never told anyone this but I voted for Bush. Honestly, Al Gore scared the hell out of me." Here was a grown man in his mid-30s afraid to publicly admit he had made a personal choice in a free election. He was afraid the other pets would attack and harm him or his family if they knew he had exercised his freedom of expression and deviated from what was expected of him as a black person.

I find it sad there is an unseen leash or cage around an entire race. Tell me of another race expected to think and vote lockstep with their race. Whites, Asians, and Latinos do not have this mentality. While there is, of late, pressure on women, Gays and lesbians, the majority of these groups do not have an invisible leash nor do they live in a social and political kennel.

Of late I have been told, by white Liberals, that I am a traitor to my race for supporting certain ideas and issues. I laughed and said, "hmm, I thought I was free and able to think beyond my race, but you are telling me that's not true?" Of course, this shut them right up realizing how racist and dumb their remarks were. Liberal whites believe, "Black people are only free to think how they expect them to." Just recently, former Vice President and presidential candidate Joe Biden said on a Black talk show, if we had a problem deciding between him and the Republican candidate, as he put it: "you ain't Black!" The sad thing is this pet mentality works against the advancement of any ethnicity or race of people. No people are free that are not free to think and act out of fear of repression and reprisal. The fear is real.

While most immigrants coming to the country work or study hard to get ahead, see their posterity advance beyond them, and to be free thinkers, "Black Pets" are taught they cannot succeed unless their Democrat and Leftists masters meet their needs and the other pets approve. They are conditioned to be happy being stroked, told how special and wonderful they are, and how badly Republicans and conservatives want to treat them. They are also taught how sorry Democrats and Progressives feel for them. If they behave and do their bidding, they will get whatever those entities feed them for their good behavior.

This conditioning, to look to others for our livelihood and affirmation has been, to me, the single most detrimental factor stifling black advancement. Think about this, the greatest advancement among black Americans, as a race, occurred under the period known as Jim Crow. Yes, you heard me right! This is the period after Emancipation and the Civil War when black codes and strict segregationist policies were enacted against black Americans. Booker T. Washington, George Washington Carver, the Tuskegee Airmen, Dr. Charles Drew, Bessie Coleman, Jesse Owens, Joe Lewis, Jackie Robinson, Jim Brown, Wilma Rudolph, Ralph Bunch, Edward Brooks, and so many more, great men and women in every field, refused to buy into the notion that their color was a barrier. They were at the top of their field and game.

It was after the end of Jim Crow, the enactment of the Civil Rights Act of 1964 and the push for Lyndon B. Johnson's "Great Society" programs, (when things should have gotten easier) we began to go backwards. As things got easier, we gave up on our work ethic to prove we were, or could be equal, even superior, to others in certain areas, to prove we deserved a shot at all there was to be achieved; not based on our color, but on our abilities and our work ethic. Somehow, somewhere along the way, "Black Power" became black inability. Add to this the rise of "White Guilt" and certain entities saw an opportunity to masses of both the Black and White race.

Some time ago I received a revelation. The best way to control society for generations and have your children and theirs to rule, is to convince others they cannot compete and do not need to try; basically, a two-step strategy. In the case of conditioning minorities, particularly black Americans, it went as follows.

1) Convince them there are certain people (Conservatives, primarily white) who are working constantly to keep them oppressed and they can therefore, never win, no matter how hard they try to compete.
2) Convince them they do not need to compete because WE are your friend and will take care of you for just existing, oh and keeping us in power.

This is precisely what has happened. The "Ruling Class," both Democrat and Republican (I cannot leave them out) Parties have adopted this strategy. The "Ruling Class" perpetuates the lie that certain minorities, Blacks, Latinos, women, and others cannot get a fair shake no matter how hard they work or try; and if they give them the power to HELP, they can have an easy life. It is a "Big Lie," but one which has been all too successful. Beginning with the "Great Society" programs, under Lyndon B. Johnson, both Parties have continually increased the size and scope of government programs. From welfare and public housing to affirmative action, quotas, lower educational requirements, free meal programs, special home lending rules and more. There has been a continual increase in social service programs which take self-reliance away and replace it with government control.

By the way, this has recently been expanded, particularly from Democrats, to include any and everyone, willing to give them power.

This is not the first time this has occurred. In 1 Samuel 8:4-19 the prophet Samuel warned Israel against wanting the ruling class to provide for them.

⁴ Then all the elders of Israel gathered themselves together, and came to Samuel unto Ramah,

*⁵ And said unto him, Behold, thou art old, and thy sons walk not in thy ways: now **make us a king** to judge us like all the nations.*

⁶ But the thing displeased Samuel, when they said, Give us a king to judge us. And Samuel prayed unto the Lord.

⁷ And the Lord said unto Samuel, Hearken unto the voice of the people in all that they say unto thee: for they have not rejected thee, but they have rejected me, that I should not reign over them.

⁸ According to all the works which they have done since the day that I brought them up out of Egypt even unto this day, wherewith they have forsaken me, and served other gods, so do they also unto thee.

⁹ Now therefore hearken unto their voice: howbeit yet protest solemnly unto them and shew them the manner of the king that shall reign over them.

¹⁰ And Samuel told all the words of the Lord unto the people that asked of him a king.

¹¹ And he said, This will be the manner of the king that shall reign over you: He will take your sons, and appoint them for himself, for his chariots, and to be his horsemen; and some shall run before his chariots.

¹² And he will appoint him captains over thousands, and captains over fifties; and will set them to plow his ground, and to reap his harvest, and to make his instruments of war, and instruments of his chariots.

¹³ And he will take your daughters to be confectionaries, and to be cooks, and to be bakers.

¹⁴ And he will take your fields, and your vineyards, and your olive yards, even the best of them, and give them to his servants.

¹⁵ And he will take the tenth of your seed, and of your vineyards, and give to his officers, and to his servants.

¹⁶ And he will take your menservants, and your maidservants, and your goodliest young men, and your asses, and put them to his work.

¹⁷ He will take the tenth of your sheep: and ye shall be his servants.

¹⁸ And ye shall cry out in that day because of your king which ye shall have chosen you; and the Lord will not hear you in that day.

¹⁹ Nevertheless the people refused to obey the voice of Samuel; and they said, Nay; but we will have a king over us.
1 Samuel 8:4-19 (KJV)

In modern terms, the admonition of giving too much power to "the king", in our day the government, it means they will tell your people where to work, when and whom to fight, and take your earning in taxes. Like the people of Israel in that day, America and the rest of the free world is, it appears ready to relinquish their rights and worth to government, in exchange for peace and safety. The problem with this is trading freedom for peace and safety will result in losing all three. The reason for this is the more power we give and the more we expect, the less we are willing to keep for ourselves. Apathy and frankly laziness will rot the society, first as individuals and eventually the nation from within. As government increases it's power, the worse the quality of life becomes.

Both Frederick Douglas and Booker T. Washington saw the potential for this slip into apathy by future generations, the loss of a healthy work ethic and a deterioration of understanding what real liberty involved. They mentioned it in a not so gentle manner in their speeches.

In an excerpt from his speech to the Massachusetts Anti-slavery Society, 1865; Frederick Douglas said:

"The American people have always been anxious to know what they shall do with us. Gen. Banks was distressed with solicitude as to what he should do with the Negro. Everybody has asked the question, and they learned to ask it early of the abolitionists, "What shall we do with the Negro?" I have had but one answer from the beginning. Do nothing with us! Your doing with us has already played the mischief with us. Do nothing with us! If the apples will not remain on the tree of their own strength, if they are worm eaten at the core, if they are early ripe and disposed to fall, let them fall! I am not for tying or fastening them on the tree in any way, except by nature's plan, and if they will not stay there, let them fall. **And if the Negro cannot stand on his own legs, let him fall also. All I ask is, give him a chance to stand on his own legs! Let him alone! If you see him on his way to school, let him alone, don't disturb him! If you see him going to the dinner table at a hotel, let him go! If you see him going to the ballot- box, let him alone, don't disturb him! If you see him going into a work-shop, just let him alone - your interference is doing him a positive injury.** *Gen. Banks' "preparation" is of a piece with this attempt to prop up the Negro. Let him fall if he cannot stand alone! If the Negro cannot live by the line of eternal justice, so beautifully pictured to you*

71

in the illustration used by Mr. Phillips, the fault will not be yours, it will be his who made the Negro, and established that line for his government. Let him live or die by that. If you will only untie his hands, and give him a chance, I think he will live."

In a speech as part of the Harvard commencement activities in 1896, Booker T. Washington said:

"This country demands that every race measure itself by the American Standard. By it, a race must rise or fall, succeed or fail, and in the last analysis mere sentiment counts for little.

*During the next half century and more, my race must continue passing through the severe American crucible. We are to be tested in our patience, our forbearance, our perseverance, our power to endure wrong, to withstand temptations, to economize, to acquire and use skill,; our ability to compete, to succeed in commerce, to disregard the superficial for the real, the appearance for the substance, to be great and yet small, learned and yet simple, high and yet the servant of all. This, **this is the passport to all that is best in the life of our republic, and the negro must possess it, or be debarred.**"*

Unfortunately, we have allowed ourselves to be trained to accept the kennel (free or easy food, housing, gifts) thinking, instead of finding a better life of liberty in fighting through the crucible. So many descendants of ex-slaves have allowed themselves to become pets and as BTW called it "debarred" from the real blessings of all that America has to offer.

I have never been opposed to true "affirmative action," as it was initially intended. I prefer, as George W. Bush called them, "affirmative access" programs. I am, however, opposed to what they became; tokenism and giving things based not upon merit, rather just to fill a quota or to pretend fairness. Unfortunately, these programs have become incentive, if not a license, to underachieve. They have also become an unfair obstacle to overachieving individuals and races, such as Asians and men in many cases.

My children are Quadroon. That is one fourth black. One day in the 8th grade my oldest son came home from school and asked "Dad, they asked on this form at school what race or color I am. What do I put down?" I told him, "whichever one opens the door the widest and fastest TODAY. Tomorrow is another day and we will have to reconsider." However, I added, "once you are in, prove that you belonged there, regardless of how you got there." In other words, you were always qualified and deserved the position regardless of your color, sex, or national origin. His eyes got big and with a huge smile he turned and ran out of the room; I knew he got it. He, as the rest of my children, have achieved far beyond myself, who achieved far beyond my father and mother, who taught me how to fight through adversity and succeed.

The reason I do not have an issue with using one's race, nationality, age or sex, for advancement, is that it is no different than using one's parental connection, school or fraternal connection, or the many other "good ol' boy and girl" networks which exist. The key is making sure the individual is worthy of the position they are being given - all other things being equal.

Let me close this chapter by saying the turning of people into pets is no longer only reserved for black people. Hispanics, women, the elderly, immigrants, all are being turned into pets. It is a crazy time and a sad situation. People are willing to give up freedom of thought and action to become pets. Many have given up their freedom of thought and expression in exchange for having things given to them, or from fear of having things taken away. Many prefer to receive free things vs. working hard and earning them. While this is a growing problem among all races, it is especially sad for the Black community considering our history. Let's stay free and continue to work to set the pets free to regain their humanity.

Chapter 10
BOOKER T. WASHINGTON

O f all the Black icons and famous figures in the short history of this nation, none shines brighter, yet is more invisible than Booker T. Washington. In fact, with the exception of the fictional character, "Uncle Tom," no other black figure has been more mischaracterized and disparaged than Booker T. Washington.

I must confess that until I happened to meet one of his great granddaughters in Washington, DC some years ago, I too had no real knowledge of the stature of this man. Before I get to his story in more detail, here are just a few bullet points on his achievements and honors.

- Founder and first head of Tuskegee Normal School, now Tuskegee University
- First Black person to receive an honorary PhD from Dartmouth College (now University), after receiving an honorary master's degree from Harvard College.
- First Black person to be invited to dine in the White House, with Theodore Roosevelt President of The United States.
- First Black person to be invited to dine with the Queen of England (Victoria) and the King of Denmark (Frederik VII)
- First Black person to grace American money (half dollar), first black person to be featured on a stamp, and first Black person to have a naval vessel named after him.

So, how is it that a personage of his stature is relatively unheard of or unspoken of in our nation today? Most young people, of all colors, have little to NO knowledge o Booker T. Washington and older non-Black individuals confuse him with George Washington Carver. His treatment by the majority of black Americans today is even worse. Many have been conditioned to believe Dr. Washington was a race traitor (Uncle Tom) or worse.

Booker Taliaferro Washington was born in a little shack on the Burroughs, slave plantation in Franklin County, Virginia, where his mother was the plantation cook. While he never knew the exact month or year of his birth, the chosen date of birth was April 5th, 1856. Booker also never knew who his birth father was, though it was believed he was the white owner or son of the owner of a nearby plantation. Whoever he was, he never played a role in his life. Booker, did not learn his mother named him Booker Taliaferro until years later. Taliaferro was an Italian name meaning Iron cutter. He had no last name and adopted the name Washington as his last name in honor of the founder and first president of our nation, George Washington.

Early life was hard on the plantation as Booker recounted in his autobiography, *Up From Slavery. He* wrote:

> *"I cannot recall a single instance during my childhood or early boyhood when our entire family sat down to the table together, God's blessing was asked, and the family ate a meal in a civilized manner. On the plantation in Virginia and even later, meals were gotten to the children very much as dumb animals got theirs. It was a piece of bread here and a scrap of meat there. It was a cup of milk at one time and some potatoes at another."*

While on the Burroughs plantation young Booker, not allowed to attend school himself, was charged with carrying the books of one of the Burroughs' daughters. It was there, standing outside the schoolhouse classroom that Booker developed a love for learning. Somehow, even to his young mind, he understood that education was what made white people better than non-whites. It was as though there was some magic in education which transformed people into a wealthier, more powerful class of society. He knew he wanted this more than anything else.

Shortly following the end of the Civil War in 1865, he recalled a man arriving on the plantation to read the Emancipation Proclamation and declare the slaves free. Booker, now nine years old recalled much shouting and celebration accompanying the event.

Sometime after Booker's birth, his mother met and married a slave named Wash Ferguson, from a nearby plantation. Ferguson had fled his plantation earlier and settled in Malden, West Virginia, a free state. Once they were free to do so, Booker, his mother and his siblings moved to Malden, West VA to join Wash, who had found employment at a salt mine there. In Malden, young Booker tried working in the mines, but realized he was not cut out for it. His real passion was for learning and this drove him. Since his family needed him to help bring an income, however, Booker agreed to work in the mines from 4am until school began and return to the mines after school ended. For some reason, possibly seeing the promise in this young boy, the wife of the mine owner Mrs. Viola Rufner, asked Booker to become her "house boy." She also allowed young Booker to get one hour of education daily. Mrs. Rufner was a very strict and demanding boss whose iron hand caused Booker to run away a few times. Mrs. Rufner took him back each time he returned. It was the strict discipline, attention to detail and follow through impressed upon Booker by Mrs. Rufner, that taught him the discipline he would later practice and use to get into and excel at Hampton Normal School and later install in the staff and students of Tuskegee Normal school, making that institution an overwhelming success.

At age 16, Booker heard of an institution of learning for ex-slaves in Hampton, Virginia. It became his dream and desire to attend Hampton Normal School, the equivalent of a vocational technical high school today. After some convincing of family and friends and a promise to return and start a school in Malden after finishing at Hampton, the community raised money for him to make the trip to Hampton. Booker set off on the 385 mile journey, but having underestimated the length and expense of the trip he ran out of funds before he reached Hampton. Booker stopped a few days to earn money in Richmond and while there slept on the streets under a raised sidewalk. He ended up having to walk the final 77 miles of his trip.

Booker arrived from Richmond, as he put it, "with a surplus of 50 cents in my pocket." Upon his arrival at Hampton Normal School, he met the lady principal and was told they would have to decide upon his acceptance. For his entrance exam, he was asked to clean a large room while waiting for a decision. Booker cleaned the room in the manner Mrs. Ruffner had taught him. Leaving it spotless and following an inspection, a young 16 year old Booker T. Washington was admitted to Hampton Normal School. This would mark the beginning of the next chapter in a particularly important life. Booker T. Washington finished at the top of his class, and ahead of schedule.

Booker kept his promise and returned to Malden, WV to open a school for the children there. However, his dream had evolved into becoming a minister and following the establishment of the school in Malden, Booker left for the nation's capital, Washington, DC, to attend Wayland Seminary. Shortly after his arrival at the seminary he became disillusioned with what he experienced. He was not disappointed in the education at the seminary, but rather in the students. According to Washington, he observed young students who hardly had any money use the little they had to rent fancy carriage rides, dressed in tuxedos, to give the impression they were more important than they were. This experience deeply influenced Booker, giving him a negative opinion of certain aspects of Black clergy, an opinion he maintained for the rest of his life.

While he was a spiritual person, reading and praying daily as well as encouraging everyone to read and pray, his opinion of many black ministers and their relationship to the scripture and their congregations was less than admirable.

Washington did not turn his back on or lose his love and zeal for the Christian faith, nor the church, Black or mainstream, he simply realized life as a minister was not for him. He felt people needed more than biblical preaching to reach their full potential. Booker maintained relationships among leaders in the Black church and spoke at church conventions and other functions. Upon hearing that Booker had left the seminary, Gen. Samuel Armstrong, the founder of the Hampton school and Booker's lifelong mentor, invited him to return to Hampton as an instructor. It was here Booker T. Washington proved himself to be the man he became.

The U.S. Army was so impressed with the success of Hampton School's training of ex-slaves, that they asked Gen. Armstrong to start a program, training Native American students. Armstrong chose Booker T. Washington to head up the program, which he was a great success at.

One event which showed the dedication and self-sacrifice Booker displayed was, when one of the Native American students became ill and needed to be treated at a government hospital in Washington, DC.

Booker was asked to accompany the student to DC and after a day's journey they stopped overnight in the city of Richmond, VA. When they went to get a hotel room Booker was informed the native student could stay there, BUT because he was Negro, he was not allowed to stay at the hotel. Without any hesitation, Booker made sure the student was secure in his room, before seeking shelter in a nearby barn. In the morning he met the student at the hotel and together they continued their journey to DC.

Booker's faithfulness, discipline and commitment endeared him the founder and headmaster of the Hampton Normal School, Gen. Samuel Armstrong, (US Army Retired). Dr. Armstrong saw something in the young Booker that Mrs. Burroughs must have seen years earlier, what this special young man could be and could achieve.

In 1881 a Black community leader in Tuskegee, Alabama wanted a school like Hampton to be built in their community. With a pledge to secure startup funding from a state legislature candidate, if the community supported his campaign, they requested a headmaster be sent from Hampton. They expected General Armstrong to send a white man, but he said he had the perfect person and sent Booker T. Washington. Booker was elated at the opportunity and expected there would be something to build upon. However, when he arrived, he found nothing was there. No buildings, no land, and no money to purchase them. The promised funds provided by the state legislature were for salaries only and not for land or buildings.

Booker T. was able to secure a shanty donated by a local church and purchased 100 acres for the school with a loan from Hampton's treasury. On July 4th, 1881 Booker T. Washington, his initial staff and his first class of students along with local citizens of both races, celebrated the opening of the Tuskegee Normal and Industrial Institute. The staff and students would go on to build all the buildings and facilities of the school. Booker T. Washington and Tuskegee became known worldwide and Native American students, as well as students from Europe, Africa, the Caribbean, and Japan, came to study at Tuskegee. Booker's public speaking was also much sought after.

While Booker T. Washington was heralded by many worldwide there were those, primarily, Democrat politicians and others in the Jim Crow south, who were not impressed by him. They in fact saw him as a threat to them and their "racist" hold on power in the south.

Sadly, not only did Booker T. Washington face opposition from southern whites, he also had a constant struggle with elements of the Black community. Chief among these black detractors was W.E.B. DuBois. DuBois wrote a book in 1903, "The Souls Of Black Folk," in which he directly attacked Washington and accused him of being a "sellout." Washington had given a speech in 1895, at the "Atlanta And Cotton States Exposition," which was heralded around the world as one of the greatest speeches ever delivered. DuBois, however, dubbed the speech the "Atlanta Compromise". According to DuBois, Washington decided to compromise on integration to placate Southern Whites to the detriment of Black folks. Sadly, to this day, the speech has become known as the "Atlanta Compromise" speech. I am familiar with the speech and Booker T. Washington's thoughts - to the point where I see NO compromise. Only the undiscerning individuals who have disparaged the name "Uncle Tom," would imagine a compromise. I am of the opinion DuBoise was just a petty envious person who resented the fact an "uneducated", former slave could have such influence in the nation and in the world, while he had little to none. Below is the Atlanta speech. Please note his warning to both races as well as the lack of any compromise. Sadly, it appears his speech was as much a prophetic message as it was a speech.

"Mr. President and Gentlemen of the Board of Directors and Citizens: One third of the population of the South is of the Negro race. No enterprise seeking the material, civil, or moral welfare of this section can disregard this element of our population and reach the highest success. I but convey to you, Mr. President and Directors, the sentiment of the masses of my race when I say that in no way have the value and manhood of the American Negro been more fittingly and generously recognized than by the

managers of this magnificent Exposition at every stage of its progress. It is a recognition that will do more to cement the friendship of the two races than any occurrence since the dawn of our freedom.

Not only this, but the opportunity here afforded will awaken among us a new era of industrial progress. Ignorant and inexperienced, it is not strange that in the first years of our new life we began at the top instead of at the bottom; that a seat in Congress or the state legislature was more sought than real estate or industrial skill; that the political convention or stump speaking had more attractions than starting a dairy farm or truck garden.

A ship lost at sea for many days suddenly sighted a friendly vessel. From the mast of the unfortunate vessel was seen a signal, "Water, water; we die of thirst!" The answer from the friendly vessel at once came back, "Cast down your bucket where you are." A second time the signal, "Water, water; send us water!" ran up from the distressed vessel, and was answered, "Cast down your bucket where you are." And a third and fourth signal for water was answered, "Cast down your bucket where you are." The captain of the distressed vessel, at last heeding the injunction, cast down his bucket and it came up full of fresh, sparkling water from the mouth of the Amazon River. To those of my race who depend on bettering their condition in a foreign land or who underestimate the importance of cultivating friendly relations with the Southern white man who is their next door neighbor, I would say: "Cast down your bucket where you are"- cast it down in making friends in every manly way of the people of all races by whom we are surrounded.

Cast it down in agriculture, mechanics, in commerce, in domestic service, and in the professions. And in this connection it is well to bear in mind that whatever other sins the South may be called to bear, when it comes to business, pure and simple, it is in the South that the Negro is given a man's chance in the commercial world, and in nothing is this Exposition more eloquent than in emphasizing this chance. Our greatest danger is that in the great leap from slavery to freedom we may overlook the fact that the masses of us are to live by the productions of our hands, and fail to keep in mind that we shall prosper in proportion as we learn to dignify and glorify common labor, and put brains and skill into the common occupations of life; shall prosper in proportion as we learn to draw the line between the superficial and the substantial, the ornamental gewgaws of life and the useful. No race can prosper till it learns that there is as much dignity in tilling a field as in writing a poem. It is at the bottom of life we must begin, and not at the top. Nor should we permit our grievances to overshadow our opportunities.

To those of the white race who look to the incoming of those of foreign birth and strange tongue and habits for the prosperity of the South sere I permitted I would repeat what I say to my own race "Cast down your bucket here you are." Cast it down among the eight millions of Negroes whose habits you know, whose fidelity and love you have tested in days when to have proved treacherous meant the ruin of your firesides. Cast down your bucket among these people who have, without strikes and labor wars, tilled your fields, cleared your forests, built your railroads and cities, and brought forth treasures from the bowels of the earth, and helped make possible this magnificent representation of the progress of the South. Casting down your bucket among my people, helping and encouraging them as you are doing on these grounds, and to education of head, hand, and heart, you will find that they will buy your surplus land, make blossom the waste places in your fields, and run your factories. While doing this, you can be sure in the future, as in the past, that you and your families will be surrounded by the most patient, faithful, law-abiding, and unresentful people that the world has seen. As we have proved our loyalty to you in the past. in nursing your children, watching by the sick-bed of your mothers and fathers, and often following them with tear-dimmed eyes to their graves, so in the future, in our humble way, we shall stand by you with a devotion that no foreigner can approach, ready to lay down our lives, if need be, in defense of yours. interlacing our industrial, commercial, civil, and religious life with yours in a way that shall make the interests of both races one. In all things that are purely social we can be as separate as the fingers, yet one as the hand in all things essential to mutual progress.

There is no defense or security for any of us except in the highest intelligence and development of all. If anywhere there are efforts tending to curtail the fullest growth of the Negro, let these efforts be turned into stimulating, encouraging, and making him the most useful and intelligent citizen. Effort or means so invested will pay a thousand percent interest. These efforts will be twice blessed--"blessing him that gives and him that takes." There is no escape through law of man or God from the inevitable: The laws of changeless justice bind Oppressor with oppressed; And close as sin and suffering joined We march to fate abreast.

Nearly sixteen millions of hands will aid you in pulling the load upward, or they will pull against you the load downward. We shall constitute one-third and more of the ignorance and crime of the South, or one-third its intelligence and progress; we shall contribute one-third to the business and industrial prosperity of the South, or we shall prove a veritable body of death, stagnating, depressing, retarding every effort to advance the body politic.

Gentlemen of the Exposition, as we present to you our humble effort at an exhibition of our progress, you must not expect overmuch. Starting thirty years ago with ownership here and there of a few quilts and pumpkins and chickens (gathered from miscellaneous sources), remember the path that has led from these to the inventions and production of agricultural implements, buggies, steam-engines, newspapers, hooks, statuary, carving, paintings, the management of drug stores and banks, has not been trodden without contact with thorns and thistles, While we take pride in what we exhibit as a result of our independent efforts, we do not for a moment forget that our part in this exhibition would fall far short of your expectations but for the constant help that has come to our educational life, not only from the Southern states, but especially from Northern philanthropists, who have made their gifts a constant stream of blessing and encouragement.

The wisest among my race understand that the agitation of questions of social equality is the extremist folly, and that progress in the enjoyment of all the privileges that will come to us must be the result of severe and constant struggle rather than of artificial forcing, No race that has anything to contribute to the markets of the world is long in any degree ostracized. It is important and right that all privileges of the law be ours, but it is vastly more important that we be prepared for the exercise of these privileges. The opportunity to earn a dollar in a factory just now is worth infinitely more than the opportunity to spend a dollar in an opera-house.

In conclusion, may I repeat that nothing in thirty years has given us more hope and encouragement, and drawn us so near to you of the white race, as this opportunity offered by the Exposition: and here bending, as it were, over the altar that represents the results of the struggles of your race and mine, both starting practically empty-handed three decades ago, I pledge that in your effort to work out the great and intricate problem which God has laid at the doors of the South. you shall have at all times the patient, sympathetic help of my race; only let this be constantly in mind, that, while from representations in these buildings of the product of field, of forest, of mine, of factory, letters, and art, much good will come, yet far above and beyond material benefits will be that higher good, that, let us pray God, will come, in a blotting out of sectional differences and racial animosities and suspicions, in a determination to administer absolute justice, in a willing obedience among all classes to the mandates of law. This, this, coupled with our material prosperity, will bring into our beloved South a new heaven and a new earth.

Booker T. Washington-Atlanta Cotton States Exposition Speech; Sept. 18, 1885

It was in one half of one line of Booker T. speech, "in all things that are purely social we can be as separate as the fingers, yet one as the hand in all things essential to mutual progress", that DuBois used to claim it was a compromise. When Booker T. stated, "In all things purely social we can be separate," he was saying we did not need to share in inter-racial, social activities to succeed. It was Booker T's view we would one day achieve integration but, for the descendants of slaves to reach that stage we must first build from within our own communities. In the same speech he said: **"No race that has anything to contribute to the markets of the world is long, in any degree ostracized. It is important and right that all privileges of the law be ours, but it is vastly more important that we be prepared for the exercise of these privileges."**

He envisioned the day when, due to our knowledge and contributions to society, we could no longer be ostracized. Later in the book, "The Negro Problem", a compilation of essays by the top Black minds at the turn of the 20th century, Booker T again explained how to build a strong and successful Black society, in his essay "An Industrial Education for the Negro.".

At the time of his death in 1915, Booker T. Washington had established Tuskegee Institute as one of, if not, the most successful Historically Black Institutions of learning (HBCUs), in the nation. At his death, it had more than 100 well-equipped buildings, 1,500 students, a 200-member faculty, teaching 38 trades and professions, and a nearly $2 million endowment.

Among other things, students built their own railroad line and station within the university grounds, allowing people to travel to the site and ship bricks and other products made at the university to destinations throughout the world. According to biographer Stephen Mansfield, in 1905, Tuskegee graduated more self-made millionaires than Harvard, Princeton and Yale combined. That was MILLIONAIRES!

Among other accomplishments was the formation of the National Negro Business League (NNBL), founded in 1900 in Boston, MA. As it was formed 12 years before the Chamber of Commerce, it can be reasonably said the chamber followed his example. Hundreds of chapters were formed across the nation in the years which followed - improving the commercial and economic prosperity of the Black community. Dr. Washington believed the real issue relating to racial discrimination and overcoming it was an economic one, more than any other. The NNBL was his way of using Black economic power to reach a goal of social equality.

Interestingly, while Washington spoke of being "separate as the fingers on a hand," the NNBL featured white business leaders as its keynote speakers. Washington's book "The Negro In Business," was printed in 1907. This inspiring book told the stories of Black individuals who began with nothing yet became wealthy and powerful through ingenuity and hard work.

This was a common thread in all Dr. Washington said and did. In the Atlanta speech, he said: **"No race that has anything to contribute to the markets of the world is long in any degree ostracized. It is important and right that all privileges of the law be ours, but it is vastly more important that we be prepared for the exercise of these privileges."**

Among Booker T. Washington's lasting legacy was dubbing the "Greenwood District" of Tulsa, Oklahoma; "Black Wall Street," - acknowledging the immense success achieved by Black merchants of North Tulsa and Oklahoma.

Upon his death, to pay their respect, over 10,000 people attended his funeral in Tuskegee. In addition, letters of condolence were received from:

Charles Henderson, Governor, State of Alabama
Theodore Roosevelt, Former President of the United States
William H. Taft, Former President of the United States
Julius Rosenwald, Millionaire Philanthropist, Friend, Benefactor and Tuskegee Board member
Andrew Carnegie, Millionaire Philanthropist, Friend and Benefactor
John D Rockefeller, Millionaire Philanthropist, Friend and Benefactor
Carolyn B. Hazard, Former President Wellesley College

President Taft in his letter of condolence wrote:

"Please convey to the family of Booker T. Washington my deepest sympathy in their sorrow. His death is in what ought to be his prime, an irretrievable loss to the nation. He was one of the most powerful forces for the proper settlement of the race question that has appeared in his generation. His encouragement to make themselves individually valuable to the community, his urging upon the homely virtues, on industry, thrift and persistent use of their opportunities, with a promise of higher achievements as a reward, have done more for the Negro race than any other one factor in their progress. "I knew Booker T. Washington well and valued him highly as a friend and a patriot. He united with a singular power of eloquence and great intellectual force and a practical executive faculty, a saving commonsense which made him the great man he was."

Much has been written and said about Booker T. Washington and there is so much more that can be written and said about the man. Unfortunately, much of what has been said, since his death, is negative, particularly in the civil rights era. It appears that of late more and more people are awakening to the immense wisdom and common sense he brought to an incredibly difficult time. His life's mission was the uplift of the descendants of Africa slaves.

This was Booker T. Washington.

Chapter 11
BLACK LIBERALISM

W e hear the terms conservatives and liberals thrown about in political discussions on a regular basis, but for the longest time, we only seemed to apply the terms to "white" people. Today the conversation has broadened to include the "Black Conservative". It is strange, however, that we never hear much about the "Black Liberal."

It is my belief that in this discussion, instead of going back to find an origin to "Black Conservatism," we need to go back to find the origins "Black Liberalism." Looking at the historical evidence, the descendants of African slaves in America have always tended to be conservative. There have been no greater patriots, no more loyal citizens, and no more of a consistently faith-oriented people in the history of this nation. Nevertheless, to hear the talk today, "the Black Conservative" is a rare new breed and a detriment and traitor of the race.

While the discussion of black conservatives and black liberals seems like a relatively new one, dating back only to the elections of 2000 or shortly before, the origins of the debate between black conservatives and black liberals traces back 100 years to the turn of the 20th Century. It was highlighted by the juxtaposition between Booker T. Washington and W.E.B. Du Bois.

On September 18th, 1895, Booker T. Washington gave one of the greatest speeches ever given in the United States - possibly in any nation, by any man or woman of any color or nationality, the afore mentioned "Cotton States Exposition" speech. So powerful was this speech that (from the very next day) for weeks the name Booker T. Washington and "the speech" were discussed on every corner and reported on the front pages of major newspaper across America and the entire western world. The speech given before a mixed crowd of thousands (black and white) attending the Atlanta Cotton States Exposition was significant not only for what was said, but for who said it and where. A black man, an ex-slave, in the Jim Crow south, had given a speech before a mixed crowd of thousands and received a thunderous reception, and ovation from all. Whites cheered wildly while much of the black audience wept with joy. After the speech, Dr. W.E.B. Dubois sent Dr. Washington a message that read:

> *"My dear Mr. Washington let me congratulate your phenomenal success at Atlanta, it was a word fitly spoken. W.E.B. Du Bois, Wilberforce, 24 Sept. 1895."*

As congratulatory as Dr. DuBois was on September 24th of 1895, in a now famous 1903 book, *The Souls of Black Folk,* he used an entire chapter to denigrate Booker T. Washington as a sellout for the very same speech. He even renamed the speech the "Atlanta Compromise Speech," which to their shame, is how most books and resource sites today refer to it. While I would like to discuss the use of the word "compromise" in detail, I must save that for another time. My focus here will be to discuss what was different about these men and their ideologies, which caused DuBois to consider Washington a "compromiser and a sellout."

The Legacies of Du Bois & Washington

In my previous discussion on ideological origins of W.E.B. DuBois, I stated he developed his thought from the "enlightened thinkers" of the European, "postmodern," thinkers at the University of Berlin and his time at Harvard. I trace the roots of current conflict Black thought to the worldviews of Booker T. Washington and W.E.B. DuBois. That is the biblical worldview of Washington and the secular humanist worldview of DuBois. In the continuation of this discussion, I want to look at the outworking of their divergent ideologies.

DuBois was born free among middle class northern whites. Schooled by northerners, he was influenced and shaped intellectually by whites. His thinking was a product of the postmodernist philosophical thinking of Europe's greatest minds of the 18th & 19th centuries. His studies at Harvard and in Berlin taught him to believe in the supremacy of the human mind. He was preoccupied with thought and intellect. His closest friends and allies were the country's all white intellectual elites. These were the so-called progressive thinkers of the time.

While DuBois was a brilliant man and a true intellectual in his own right, the entire fabric of his persona was of a white origin. He never had the post slavery Black experience to draw from, yet he sought to think of black people and their plight and needs from his own white world.

Most of what DuBois is known for and given credit for was the work of his white colleagues, including his involvement in the founding and work at the NAACP. While DuBois is considered to have been the or even a founding member, of the NAACP he was, in reality, only the editor of their magazine and their communications director. The actual founders and original leaders of the NAACP were three "progressive" whites, Mary White Ovington, Dr. Henry Moskowitz, and William Walling. These three Republicans, were the founders of the NAACP.

Some of his notable, and close circle of friends were Roger Baldwin, founder of the ACLU and Margaret Sanger, founder of Planned Parenthood. Both were vehement opponents of America's religious and capitalist system and each fostered pure antagonism toward this nation. In addition, DuBois joined and was used by the Communist Party to attack the American capitalist system. His vision for Black ascent was by creating an intellectual elite class among Blacks.

Washington, on the other hand, was impressed with teaching on a very practical level. Born a slave among poor, black people, in the south, he was raised and educated among poor, black people, and spent the majority of his life among poor, black people. In the end it was amongst poor, black people that he was laid to rest. His education was begun by and among black people, and although he attended Hampton Institute, which was led by whites, much of the faculty and all the students were black. He loved, lived and gave his life to the uplift of black people. This practical training taught Washington to rely on his own abilities only as far as they could take him, and then to trust God to take over and make the seemingly impossible, possible. Man was not limited to what he was capable of, rather with the help of a personal and caring God, he was capable of much more.

DuBois, who was a devotee of Darwinism, presented his "Talented Tenth" model as a way to elevate the Black race, along with agitation for civil rights. This "Talented Tenth" model was nothing more than an elitist idea based upon the Darwinian theory of the "survival of the fittest." In DuBois' version of this theory, there were those within the race who were of superior breeding and intellect, and there were those who were incapable of being elevated, without the help of a superior intellect. These Black elite, these select, or fittest, who were to be the saviors of the race, were the only ones among the race worthy of attention and investment of time and energy. Theoretically, once they arrived, they would reach back and raise the rest of their race. This thought was very much that of Margaret Sanger and her idea of eugenics as weeding out the unfit. In unleashing her Negro Project, Sanger enlisted the help of DuBois and several "Talented Tenth," black pastors and leaders. In doing this she stated:

> *"The minister's work is also important and he should be trained, perhaps by the Federation as to our ideals and the goals that we hope to reach. We do not want word to go out that we want to exterminate the Negro population. The minister is the man who can straighten out that idea if it ever occurs to any of their more rebellious members."* (letter to Clarence J. Gamble, M.D.-1939)

In 1932 DuBois wrote an article entitled: *Black Folk and Birth Control*. In it, he stated that: *"The Negro must learn that among human races and groups, as among vegetables, quality and not mere quantity really counts."*

He goes on to say: *".....On the other hand, the mass of ignorant Negroes still breed carelessly and disastrously, so that the increase among Negroes, even more than the increase among whites, is from that part of the population least intelligent and fit, and least able to rear their children properly."*[1]

This belief, the "Talented Tenth" idea, was built upon something called "Popular Eugenics" and was later adopted and supported by many notable black ministers, educators and leaders - THE ELITE! Among them were:

Claude A. Barnett - Director, Associated Negro Press, Chicago Illinois
Michael J. Bent, M.D - Meharry Medical School, Nashville, Tennessee

Dr. Mary Mcleod Bethune - President, National Council of Negro Women, Washington D.C., Special advisor to President Roosevelt on minority groups, and founder of Bethune-Cookman College, Daytona Beach, Florida

Dr. Dorothy Boulding Ferebee, cum laude graduate of Tufts, President of Alpha Kappa Alpha (the nation's oldest black sorority), Washington, D.C.

Charles S. Johnson, President, Fisk University, Nashville Tennessee

Eugene Kinckle Jones, Executive Secretary, National Urban League, NY

Rev. Adam Clayton Powell Jr., Pastor, Abyssinian Baptist Church, New York

Bishop David H. Sims, Pastor, African Methodist Episcopal Church, Philadelphia, Pennsylvania

Arthur Spingarn, President, National Association for the Advancement of Colored People

Charles S. Johnson. The first black president of Fisk University wrote: "'Eugenic discrimination' was necessary for blacks."

We can add a long list of modern day black "leaders" who continue to support these notions.

Following the death of Booker T. Washington, it was thought Du Bois would take on the mantle of "unifying black leader", however, Marcus Garvey took that from him. This led to a new attack and the destruction of Garvey by DuBois and his white supporters. Garvey, a devoted follower of the teachings of Booker T. Washington was ultimately silenced by being run out of America.

Chapter 12

GEORGE WASHINGTON CARVER

A s with so many of the truly great figures, who were descendants of slaves from our past, George Washington Carver is another example of achieving greatness with no role model, "that looks like us." There was NO renowned, black scientist or professor of agriculture prior to him. He had no role model "that looked like him." He was born with a love of agriculture and he pursued his passion with faith in God to give him the wisdom and tools needed to become the leading authority in his field.

Most of us have grown up being taught about Dr. Carver (the peanut man) in grammar school, but in case there are those who do not know his story, or for those who need a refresher, here is a short biography of this great man.

Dr. Carver, like Booker T. Washington (BTW) was born a slave. Although his exact date of birth remains unknown historians believe it to be 1864. Carver was born on a plantation in Missouri and again like BTW, never knew his father. The farm was owned by a man named Moses Carver. Still a newborn George, his mother and sister were kidnapped by Confederate soldiers and sold to slave owners in Kentucky. Moses Carver sent an agent to find George, his mother and sister, but only George was recovered and returned to the Carver farm. To his credit, Moses Carver and his wife taught George and his brother to read, and Mrs. Carver insisted the boys attend school. Because he was not very strong George worked with Mrs. Carver in the kitchen and garden, while his brother James, who did not like school, preferred to work the farm with their now adopted father, Moses. Helping Mrs. Carver in the kitchen and the garden George became enamored with plants and foods. It came naturally to him and he experimented in planting and growing various plants and vegetables. At the young age of just under thirteen, George had learned to develop natural pesticides and fungicides.

It was during this time George left the farm to attend school in Kansas, and Minneapolis. He worked in kitchens to earn his keep and entered baking contests using his own original recipes and concoctions. After high school George applied to various colleges and, due to his grades and an essay he submitted, was initially accepted to Highland Presbyterian College in Kansas until he showed up and it was learned that he was Black. Imagine getting accepted to a university or job and making the effort to travel and show up, making plans surrounding this, only to be rejected upon showing up due to your skin color. Nevertheless, George pressed on and worked at several jobs, on farms, in Kansas and New Mexico, as well as working for the railroad. All of this time, however, he never gave up on his dream and plan. George saved his money and continued to look for a college that would accept him.

At the age of 24, George finally found a school that would accept him, Simpson College in Iowa. Strangely George majored in music and art at Simpson, hoping to become a teacher. One of the instructors at Simpson recognized his love for plants and flowers in his art and encouraged him to apply to the agriculture school at Iowa State Agricultural School, which is now Iowa State University. At Iowa Ag, George flourished getting not only a bachelor's degree (the first Black American ever to do so at the school) but a master's degree in 1896. He was so impressive that while working for his master's degree he became DIRECTOR of the Iowa State Experimental Station, where he discovered two types of fungi which were named after him (imagine that as a good thing). Here George became a leading agricultural scientist and developed what he would later become famous for, crop rotation.

As the young Dr. Carver was developing his craft and skill, another young black educator was making a name for himself. Booker T. Washington recognized the special gift Dr. Carver had and reached out to him inviting him to develop an agriculture department at Tuskegee Institute. This by the way was in 1896, the same year in which Booker T. Washington delivered his most famous "Atlanta Exposition" speech, which propelled him to international prominence.

Building a great name, prestige and the potential for earning lots of money, Dr. Carver could have remained at Iowa Agricultural School, or accepted offers from major universities in the east, but he instead accepted the invitation of Booker T. Washington to join the faculty of Tuskegee, where he would spend the remainder of his life.

As opposed to the "Talented Tenth" philosophy of W.E.B. Dubois, Dr. Carver chose the Frederick Douglas, Booker T. Washington path, that a people and nation are only as strong as their common people. It is not at the top, but at the bottom, that a foundation is built. Dr. Carver chose to give his time and life to help the poor farmers and people of the south, most of whom were black and descendants of African slaves.

Later in life Dr. George Carver added Washington to his name in honor of his hero and the man who gave him his place at Tuskegee, Booker T. Washington.

One of the interesting things about Dr. Carver is that although he discovered and invented numerous methods and techniques related to farming and plants, he never patented any of his discoveries or inventions. He said, "One reason I never patent my products is that if I did it would take so much time, I would get nothing else done. But mainly I don't want my discoveries to benefit specific favored persons."

While this extraordinary life and the circumstances of it are fairly well known, what is less known is Dr. George Washington Carver's spiritual life. George Washington Carver was a deeply spiritual man, who lived his faith. He stated his experience of coming to Christ and that relationship this way: **"Never since, have I been without this consciousness of the Creator speaking to me. The out of doors has been to me more and more a great cathedral in which God could be continuously spoken to and heard from."**

Of his conversion to Christianity Dr. Carver wrote:

"I was just a mere boy when converted, hardly ten years old. There isn't much of a story to it. God just came into my heart one afternoon while I was alone in the 'loft' of our big barn while I was shelling corn to carry to the mill to be ground into meal.

97

A dear little white boy, one of our neighbors, about my age came by one Saturday morning, and in talking and playing he told me he was going to Sunday School tomorrow morning. I was eager to know what a Sunday school was. He said they sang hymns and prayed. I asked him what prayer was and what they said. I do not remember what he said, I only remember that as soon as he left I climbed up into the 'loft,' knelt down by the barrel of corn and prayed as best I could. I do not remember what I said. I only recall that I felt so good that I prayed several times before I quit. My brother and myself were the only colored children in that neighborhood and of course, we could not go to church, Sunday school, or school of any kind. So, alone in that barn was my simple conversion, and I have tried to keep the faith."

> *G. W. Carver; July 24, 1931*
> *Letter to Isabelle Coleman*

Other quotes revealing Dr. Carver's deep faith are:

"...to me, my dear young friends, nature in its varied forms are little windows through which God permits me to continue to commune with Him, and to see much of His glory, majesty, and power by simply lifting the curtain and looking in."

"I never have to grope for methods. The method is revealed at the moment I am inspired to create something new... Without God to draw aside the curtain I would be helpless."

"God is going to reveal to us things He never revealed before if we put our hands in His. No books ever go into my laboratory. The thing I am to do and the ways of doing it are revealed to me."

"Fear of something is at the root of hate for others and hate within will eventually destroy the hater."

One of his more humorous quotes is: **"When I was young, I said to God, 'God, tell me the mystery of the universe.' But God answered, 'That knowledge is for me alone.' So, I said, 'God, tell me the mystery of the peanut.' Then God said, 'Well George, that's more nearly your size.' And he told me."**

At the time of his death, as the result of an injury suffered from a fall, Dr. Carver had saved over $60,000 which is the equivalent of over $1 million today. He dedicated it to a museum at Tuskegee to showcase his work, hoping to inspire others to look into and build upon his work.

Little is ever mentioned of the Tuskegee millionaires created in the early 1900s. Most of these were farmers who learned from Drs. Carver and Washington, who built successful farms and ranches with what they learned in the classroom and about life at the Tuskegee Institute.

Again, like Frederick Douglas, Booker T. Washington and so many of the heroes of Black America, George Washington Carver was a man of faith whom God raised up at a pivotal time to help his people, his nation, AND the entire world. We do well to remember him and his legacy.

Chapter 13

THE NATION OF ISLAM

O ne of the most notable and increasingly influential entities to rise during the civil rights movement in America is the Nation of Islam (NOI), formerly known as the "Black Muslims." Interestingly, as often as we hear about the NOI, few know their history or who they really are. They are esteemed and feared by many, yet strangely few seem to actually care enough to investigate their history, theology and rise in prominence. I want to change this, in hopes it might remove much of the awe and mystery behind the "cult." Yes, I said cult.

While the members are exclusively black, other than sharing the name they have nothing in common with Islam or Muslims around the world. The NOI is more like the "Christian Identity"[1] movement is to Christianity. I guess we could call it the "Islamic Identity" movement. Each takes elements of their namesake faith, mixes it with convenient, dreamed up fables, and mis-shapes it into an ethnocentric aberration that bears little resemblance to the Christian or Islamic faith. Both cults have the common thread of an intrinsic hatred of other ethnicities, united particularly in a hatred of Jews.

Let's look at the history of the "Nation of Islam."

Prior to the Nation of Islam, there was another "Black Muslim" group called the Moorish Science Temple Of America (MST). The Moorish Science Temple was initially called the Moorish Temple of Science until a slight name change a few years later. Prior to this the MST was the Canaanite Temple founded in Newark, New Jersey in 1913 by an individual named Timothy Drew. Drew changed his name to Noble Drew Ali and moved the group to Chicago. In 1929 Drew was arrested on suspicion of murder of a rival MST leader but never charged. Shortly after his release Drew himself died. A year later a prominent MST member, Wallace Fard, known in the MST as David Ford-El, appeared in Detroit as Wallace Fard Muhammad.

Found on the NOI website under: "Brief History on Origin of the Nation of Islam," it states:

"On July the Fourth, the day of America's Independence celebration, He announced the beginning of His mission which was to restore and to resurrect His lost and found people, who were identified as the original members of the Tribe of Shabazz from the Lost Nation of Asia. The lost people of the original nation of African descent, were captured, exploited, and dehumanized to serve as servitude slaves of America for over three centuries. His mission was to teach the downtrodden and defenseless Black people a thorough Knowledge of God and of themselves, and to put them on the road to Self-Independence with a superior culture and higher civilization than they had previously experienced.

The "he" spoken of refers to Wallace Fard Muhammad known as "The Master" by followers of the teachings of the NOI. The NOI website goes on to say:

"He taught us the ways of love and peace, of truth and beauty. We are being led into the path of a new spiritual culture and civilization of complete harmony and peace, one of refinement in the pursuit of happiness and eternal joy in the Supreme Knowledge of God and the Science of everything in life."

"IN 1931, THE MASTER WAS preaching this Great Truth of salvation when He met a man named Elijah Poole in Detroit, Michigan. He chose him to be His Divine Representative in continuing this most difficult task of bringing truth and light to His lost and found people. For 3 1/2 years He taught and trained the Honorable Elijah Muhammad night and day in the profound Secret Wisdom of the Reality of God, which included the hidden knowledge of the original people who were the first founders of civilization on our Planet and who had full knowledge of the Universal Order of Things from the beginning of the Divine Creation.

Upon the Master's departure in 1934, the Honorable Elijah Muhammad labored tirelessly to bring life to his mentally and spiritually dead people until his return to the Master in 1975. The Honorable Elijah Muhammad identified the Master as being the answer to the one that the world had been expecting for the past 2,000 years under the names Messiah, the second coming of Jesus, the Christ, Jehovah, God, and the Son of Man. When the Honorable Elijah Muhammad asked Him to identify Himself He replied that He was the Mahdi. He signed His name in 1933 as Master Wallace Fard Muhammad to express the meaning of One who had come in the Early Morning Dawn of the New Millennium to lay the base for a New World Order of Peace and Righteousness on the foundation of Truth and Justice; to put down tyrants and to change the world into a Heaven on Earth.[2]

There is so much wrong with everything written above, I hardly know where to begin. There is also much more mind boggling narrative following this, but I will leave it to the reader to research this for themselves and ask, what in the world would cause anyone to buy into this. I think, though, the best place to begin is by looking into the so-called Master, Wallace D. Farad and "His divine representative," Elijah Poole, aka the Honorable Elijah Mohammad. We can return to some of the just plain nonsense piece by piece later.

Let's begin, however, with Wallace D. Fard, aka Wallace D. Fard, aka Wallace Fard Mohammad aka Wallace D. Ford aka Professor Ford, Mr. Farrad Mohammed, Mr. F. Mohammed Ali and as stated above David Ford-El.

W.D. Fard was truly a man of mystery. In 1959 the FBI undertook an investigation into his background and came up empty handed. From witnesses and records the FBI was unable to determine if Fard came from Hawaii, New Zealand, Los Angeles, Oregon, or Mecca, where he claimed to be from. The mystery remains unsolved to this day.

What we do know of Fard in relation to the NOI, other than some of the suspect writings of the NOI, is based largely upon the 1938 work of sociologist Erdmann Doane Beynon in the American Journal of Sociology. That is, Farad showed up in Detroit in 1930 and taught the history and doctrine of the NOI there until his disappearance in 1934. Just as mysterious as his origin, is his disappearance. Farad began his work in Detroit selling silks door to door to Black Americans who had migrated north to Detroit. As part of his sales pitch he would tell his customer the silks were from their homeland, Africa. He would pique the curiosity and interest of his customers with stories, causing them to want to know more. He would follow up his initial visit with his hosts inviting guests to join, thus began the teachings of the NOI.[3]

Farad mysteriously disappeared in 1934 and was never heard from again, leading to the rise of Elijah Poole, now Elijah Mohammad, as the new leader of the Nation of Islam.

I have to say there was a great deal of mysterious dying and disappearing of these leaders.

The NOI was a fairly obscure cult resigned to the Black, inner city, ghettos of major cities for several years. Detroit, Chicago, New York City and Philadelphia were the breeding grounds for the cult. With the civil rights movement and the inner city uprisings, the Black Nationalist teachings of the NOI gained traction, particularly after the conversion to the cult by Malcolm Little who took the name Malcolm X. After Malcolm joined the group and took a prominent teaching and leadership role, the group began to receive national attention. Also, as a result of Malcolm's influence, the world heavyweight champion Casius Clay converted to the NOI, taking the name Mohammed Ali and brought additional attention to the group causing a rise in its membership. Between the early 1950s and 60s , due to the ministry of Malcolm X, the cult grew from about 500 to 25,000.

As Malcolm's influence grew to rise above that of Elijah Mohammad, the division between them grew as well. In March of 1964 Malcolm X left the cult after an ever growing divide between himself and Elijah Mohammad. After a pilgrimage to Mecca, Malcolm rejected the teachings of Elijah Mohammad, the NOI and their racial superiority doctrine, to embrace traditional Sunni Islam. He took the name Malik El-Shabazz.

Though Malcolm had opposed and spoke openly against other civil rights leaders such as Martin Luther King Jr., he sought to unite with them after his conversion.

On January 21st, 1965, Malik El-Shabazz was assassinated while preparing to give a public speech in the Audubon Ballroom in New York

City. In an interview two days earlier, Malik said the Nation of Islam was actively trying to kill him. While that was never proven, most believe that is exactly what happened.

After the assassination of Malcolm X, eventually Louis Walcott another gifted and fiery speaker rose in prominence within the nation of Islam. Walcott, like Malcolm, had taken the last name of X. After Malcolm's death, Walcott changed his last name to Farrakhan and became the new dynamic face of the NOI.

Following the death of Elijah Mohammad, Wallace D. Mohammad, the son of Elijah Mohammad, took over the leadership as the Supreme Minister of the NOI. Wallace desired to move away from the ethnocentric and racist views of his father and the NOI, moving it toward the more orthodox Sunni strain of Islam. This led to a growing rift between Farrakhan and Wallace Mohammad, which eventually led to a split and Farrakhan leaving to bring the NOI back to the original teachings of Black superiority as espoused by Wallace D. Farad, and Elijah Mohammad.

Following the split and Louis Farrakhan's takeover of the NOI and with the rise of Black Nationalism, the NOI under Farrakhan grew to new heights in membership and national attention. The ultimate show of Farrakhan's popularity and influence was the "Million Man March" in 1995 with an estimated crowd size of between 400,000 and 800,000.

Tragically, many so-called black, Christian Pastors and leaders have compromised their values and their adherence to the Gospel of Christ, to align and support Farrakhan's anti-white and anti-Jewish, Black Nationalist views. As an example on July 30th, 2015 the 119-year-old, historic, Mount Zion Missionary Baptist Church, a nationally recognized historical site, provided space to the Nation of Islam for its public event. A crowd of 1500 attended to hear Minister Farrakhan say the following:

"I'm looking for 10,000 in the midst of a million. I'm looking for 10,000 in the midst of the million. Ten thousand fearless men who say death is sweeter than to continue life under tyranny. I'm looking for 10,000 in the midst of a million. I'm looking for 10,000 in the midst of the million. Ten thousand fearless men who say death is sweeter than to continue life under tyranny. Death is sweeter than to continue to live and bury our children while white folks give the killer hamburgers. Death is sweeter than watching us slaughter each other to the joy of a 400-year-old enemy. Death is sweeter. The Quran teaches persecution is worse than slaughter. Then it says, retaliation is prescribed in matters of the slain. Retaliation is a prescription from God to calm the breasts of those whose children have been slain. If the federal government will not intercede in our affairs, then we must rise up and kill those who kill us. Stalk them and kill them and let them feel the pain of death that we are feeling."

At the end of those remarks, also highlighted by Nation of Islam publication "The Final Call", the crowd of men and women clapped enthusiastically as they rose their feet, apparently in agreement with the minister's remarks. The church's pastor, the Rev. Ralph M. Ross, told The Christian Post that he was in attendance when Farrakhan gave his controversial speech, and that **he did not see anything wrong with the minister's call for retaliation,** or in his point of view and demand for justice.[4]

Farrakhan's message was so divisive and inflammatory that the Anti-Defamation League (ADL) said, "The Nation of Islam (NOI), the oldest Black Nationalist organization in the U.S., has maintained a consistent record of anti-Semitism and racism since its founding in the 1930s."

Even the ultra-liberal Southern Poverty Law Center has branded the NOI, a hate group, and says of the NOI and Farrakhan: "Louis Farrakhan heads the Nation of Islam, a group he has led since 1977 that is based on a somewhat bizarre and fundamentally anti-white theology. Farrakhan is an anti-Semite who routinely accuses Jews of manipulating the U.S. government and controlling the levers of world power."[5]

Now that we have looked at the history of the NOI, and the secular realities of the organization, let's discuss the origin of its theology and spiritual beliefs and how they line up with Christian and orthodox Christian belief.

The NOI has no official scripture, or book as their system of belief, rather they claim to believe in the Qur'an, the Bible and "The Scriptures of ALL the prophets of God." The question is who are "All" of these prophets whose Scriptures they believe in. They surely do not believe in the Judeo- Christian Bible or the Qur'an, as their teaching are galaxies away from anything resembling orthodox Judaism, Christianity or Islam. Their doctrine of the origin of the world and races is more of a mixture of mythology and fantasy. According to NOI teachings, the story of the world and of Yakub, an evil scientist who created the white race is as follows.

About 6500 years ago the entire human race was black. They were a peaceful, wonderful people except for some nebulous groups, and one evil scientist named Yakub. Yakub or Mr. Yakub, began experimenting with genetics in order to create what they hoped would be, a new super race. He would take lighter skinned children and have them mate with other lighter skinned children to create an even lighter skinned people. He eventually created a Caucasian or white race. According to the NOI magazine "The Final Call", the "history" or STORY goes as follows.

"The White man first appeared 6,000 years ago on the Island of Patmos (or Pelan), in the Aegean Sea, where they had been "made" by a 600-year process of selective breeding called "grafting." Under the command of a Black scientist named Yakub, the 59,999 Blacks who came with Yakub to the island were placed under a system of mating that was based on skin color, in which only lighter-complexioned babies were allowed to survive. Over the course of many generations the population of Patmos began to grow lighter and lighter until, after 600 years, the people became very pale with blue eyes and blonde hair. From this island-based tribe of white-skinned albinos came, a behaviorally aggressive race of rulers—namely, the Caucasians—who then spread into every corner of the world and who now represent 9 percent of the world population."[5]

They go on to say: "This teaching of the birth of the White race has been central to the belief system in the Nation of Islam."[6]

As I began this discussion of the Nation of Islam, I said it was based on mythology. The sad thing is there is so much wrong with this STORY I hardly know where to begin. The story begins with the proposition that the human race already existed prior to 6500 years ago and they were apparently black. We are not told who commissioned Yakub to create this new race, just that he was charged with the task of overseeing it. We are not told where the 59,999 people he brought to this island to create a new race came from, and it would also appear Yakub lived for over 500 years to see this commission through. NO religious tradition has any history even close to this narrative. Even traditional Islam, with which the NOI is supposed to be aligned rejects this as fantasy.

The modern doctrine of the NOI, like its Caucasian counterpart, "Christian Identity"[1], is essentially more of an ethnic, social society than a religion or faith. At its core, the real and sole doctrine is about black empowerment, which is not a bad thing in itself, but theirs stems from a root of bitterness and race hatred that fuels their fire and blinds them to the fact that there is no theological basis upon which to put one's faith, which is a shame.

Many of the NOI's secular and social ideas are actually good. Black empowerment, the emphasis on family, and leading moral lives are all wonderful things worthy to be taught and promoted. The difference in these ideas which are the same propositions put forth by Frederick Douglas, Booker T. Washington, George Washington Carver, Marcus Garvey and those of Farrakhan, are the bitterness and animosity fueling the NOI. These beliefs guarantee that the Nation of Islam and those within the organization, will never fully integrate or succeed in the greater society which is America.

Chapter 14

THE BLACK PANTHER PARTY (BPP)

I remember as a freshman in college wanting badly to join the Black Panther Party. I believed they were doing good in their communities and standing up for the injustices in the Black community. Going to school in Lubbock, Texas, however, did not lend itself to joining the BPP. I did my part though, being as radical and BLACK as I could at Texas Tech University. I was "Woke" long before there was wokeness. Now looking back, I think more than anything I just thought they were "hip" with their dress and boldness. The rest was justification.

Like the Nation of Islam, the Black Panther Party adopted many admirable goals and programs. Among them were feeding programs for children and the poor, educational programs for children, and community health clinics. The BPP also challenged the establishment, forcing them to enforce the law equally. They studied and knew the law and their rights under the law. One of the interesting things the BPP did was to exercise their 2nd amendment right to bear arms. They purchased and openly carried arms in Oakland, California. I find it ironic the BPP were the original gun activists. The tight regulation of firearms in the state of California and in many "Blue states," were begun and enacted as a result of state legislators wanting to control the ownership and use of firearms by those "Crazy Negroes."

Talk about role reversals, in 1967 it was Ronald Reagan who signed the "Mulford Act," a state Bill prohibiting the open carry of loaded firearms, along with an addendum prohibiting loaded firearms in the state Capitol, Sacramento, California. The 1967 bill took California down the path to having some of the strictest gun laws in America and helped jumpstart a surge of national gun control restrictions.

"The law was part of a wave of laws passed in the late 1960s regulating guns, especially to target African-Americans," says Adam Winkler, author of *Gunfight: The Battle Over the Right to Bear Arms*[1]. "Including the Gun Control Act of 1968, which adopted new laws prohibiting *certain people* from owning guns, providing for beefed up licensing and inspections of gun dealers and restricting the importation of Cheap "Saturday Night Specials" that were popular in some urban communities[1]."

At that time the National Rifle Association supported "gun control." Talk about role reversal. In contrast to the NRA's rigid opposition on gun control in today's America, the organization fought alongside the government for stricter gun regulations in the 1960s. This was part of an effort to keep guns out of the hands of African-Americans as racial tensions in the nation grew. The NRA felt especially threatened by the Black Panthers, whose well-photographed carrying of weapons in public spaces was entirely legal in the state of California, where they were based.

The Black Panthers were "innovators" in the way they viewed the Second Amendment at the time, says Winkler. Rather than focus on the idea of self-defense in the home, the Black Panthers brazenly took their weapons to the streets where they felt the public, particularly African-Americans needed protection from a corrupt government.

"These ideas eventually infiltrated into the NRA to shape the modern gun debate," explains Winkler. As gun control laws swept the nation, the organization adopted a similar stance to that of the activist group they once fought to regulate, with support for open-carry laws and concealed weapon laws high on their agenda. (Ibid)

Like the Nation of Islam, the Black Panther Party had many good ideas with regard to self-help and rights. However, like the NOI the BPP fell victim to a root of bitterness which developed into seeing equality, not as the act of lifting a community up, but the act of bringing others down. It became a "get whitey" strategy vs. let's join others in the shared prosperity offered to all by this nation. Also, like the NOI, the personal flaws (which I call the "Sin Nature" of mankind), that tend to manifest themselves when men attain power, prestige and influence, affected and hurt their cause.

The "Panthers" were persecuted and prosecuted by the powers that be, however, in the end they were the authors of their own demise. While they may have begun with the right idea or ideas, they ultimately lost their way.

The reason they failed, like so many after them, was aligning themselves with the false philosophy of Communist Marxism, which has been the downfall of many well-meaning individuals and entities.

This influence is seen in the Black Panther's "Ten Point Platform," authored by founders, Huey Newton and Bobby Seale. The ten points are as follows:

1. We Want Freedom. We Want Power to Determine The Destiny Of Our Black Community.
2. We Want Full Employment For Our People.
3. We Want An End To The Robbery By The Capitalists Of Our Black Community.
4. We Want Decent Housing Fit For The Shelter Of Human Beings.
5. We Want Education For Our People That Exposes The True Nature Of This Decadent American Society. We Want Education That Teaches Us Our True History And Our Role In The Present-Day Society.
6. We Want All Black Men To Be Exempt From Military Service.
7. We Want An Immediate End To Police Brutality And Murder Of Black People.
8. We Want Freedom For All Black Men Held In Federal, State, County And City Prisons And Jails.
9. We Want All Black People When Brought To Trial To Be Tried In Court By A Jury Of Their Peer Group, Or People From Their Black Communities, As Defined By The Constitution Of The United States.
10. We Want Land, Bread, Housing, Education, Clothing, Justice And Peace[1].

As has been the case with many oppressed and downtrodden people, and observed in the BPP's "Ten Points," most of these ideas are not intrinsically bad or evil. However, it is evident in some of these points that the Black Panthers chose to follow a Marxist Communist philosophy vs. American founding principles of "Free Enterprise Capitalism."

One can see the same situation throughout the world. For example, in South Africa, the ANC (African National Congress) was founded in 1912 for the purpose of uniting and giving full rights to indigenous African people and mixed race people who were being discriminated against.

After the introduction of "Apartheid" as the official national policy of South Africa in 1948, and after Capitalist Europe and America failed to support their push for equality under the direction of Nelson Mandela (who had secretly joined the Communist Party), the African national Congress Party (ANC) aligned themselves with Communism. We have seen this time after time, when in a vacuum, Socialism and Communism take root in the absence of "just" leadership and wreaks havoc in every nation and culture they invade and rule.

One of the main problems with Marxism and its derivatives Socialism and Communism, is that it, by its own admission, is godless or more correctly "without" God.

In the case of the Black Panther Party, after becoming disillusioned with everything, including communism, infighting and ultimately bad behavior, squashed any good associated with the name "Black Panthers." The leadership fell apart collectively and individually. Huey Newton was believed to have been addicted to crack cocaine, accused of murder in the case of a young 17 year old prostitute and later attempting the assassination of a witness to the murder. While he was never found guilty of the crimes, Newton was himself murdered in 1989.

Eldridge Cleaver fled the country to live in exile in Cuba, France and Algiers after a gun battle with police. He would return after several years but as a different man. Seeking religion, he moved between several faiths, fought a drug addiction, and eventually died in 1998.

Bobby Seale had the most violent history of these three prominent BPP leaders. He is most famously known for being one of the "Chicago 8" defendants accused of inciting the riot at the 1968 Democratic National Convention. He would serve four years for that conviction and was subsequently accused of two additional murders.

Seale was reported to have had a parting of ways with Huey P. Newton, over the direction of a film on the BPP. It is believed the two had a major falling out which left Seale badly beaten and in hiding for a year afterwards. Of the three main figures in the Legendary Black Panther Party, he remains the last survivor.

Time after time, lives and outcomes associated with Marxist Communism tend not to end well. Historically, neither have the lives of those living under such a systems and policies turned out for the better. In fact of late, every nation that has chosen to follow a Marxist-Communist path has gone from riches to rags or rags to worse rags. The Black panther Party, while I do believe the founders and leaders began with good intentions, succumbed to the same failings of all mankind; the "Original Sin" of the first man, Adam. Whether we like it or not, the truth remains, a society in which man is god, is a doomed society.

Chapter 15
DR. MARTIN LUTHER KING JR.

This next discussion is the most difficult for me in this entire endeavor and I am sure it will be easy to consider me a "hater or in opposition to the work of Dr. Martin Luther King Jr. I am sure that many, if not most, will not fully understand my intent in this discussion of his life and impact, which were great. No one is given (deservedly) more credit for shaping and furthering civil rights than Dr. Martin Luther King Jr. Dr. King's influence is undeniable, but how he became a powerful voice and influence amongst all the other voices of his time is not as welcome a discussion. As stated, his was not the only voice raised for the fair and equal treatment of descendants of slaves in America. Among the more prominent other voices were Stokely Carmichael, H. Rap Brown and Malcolm X. Not to mention those in political office such as Barbara Jordan and Julian Bond. While Dr. King is now a legend and has a national holiday in his name, he was not seen as the figure he is among black Americans in the midst of the intense mid-1960s.

Michael King, which was his real name, was a bold and gifted orator. He was fiercely intelligent and well ahead of his peers. He entered and studied at Morehouse College in Atlanta at the age of 15 and received a bachelor's degree in Sociology. At 19 he attended Crozer Theological Seminary in Pennsylvania, where he earned a Bachelor of Divinity degree. He then went on to receive a PhD in Theology from Boston University.

Dr. King would later publicly attribute much of his philosophy of social justice and non-violence to two people, professor and theologian Walter Rauschenbusch and Mahatma Gandhi. Privately, however, King's real influences were Bayard Rustin, Harris Wafford and Glenn Smiley. It was Rustin who organized the Southern "Freedom Rides," and the 1963 "March on Washington". Rustin a controversial figure at the time was a gifted organizer, but as a homosexual in the 40s to 60s, he had to remain in the shadows.

There have been many controversial and negative attacks upon Dr. King's personal life, but I do not want to go there. I believe Dr. King was a great and seminal figure in the history of our nation. He was one of the most gifted orators ever and had a power of influence rarely seen. However, I must question and have us look at some aspects of his life, story, and worldview, which are questionable. I am not referencing his personal actions, rather his beliefs, influences, his influence on others and on this nation. These beliefs and influences, in my opinion, have stifled the progress of Black Americans. In the end, Dr. King's priorities verged from a lack of civil rights, to a focus on more Progressive issues, an antiwar and socialist agenda.

It is my belief Dr. King was not a believer in the orthodoxy of Christianity and the Church founded upon the person of Jesus. Dr. King, like W.E.B. DuBois, used the vehicle of spirituality among Black citizens to couch his message in. Per some of his own writings, Dr. King did not believe in the divinity of Jesus, His resurrection, the ascension, salvation through the "Blood Sacrifice" of Jesus, the primacy and authority of Jewish and Christian scriptures, or a personal salvation, which are all central Christian beliefs. The miracles were also myths to Dr. King. Even his so-called coming to the altar were, per his own words, something he did for his sister and something he never actually believed in. Later, as mentioned earlier, he attributed his learning and practicing of the peaceful resistance technique primarily to Gandhi and not Jesus or any Christian person.

In the book "The Radical King," Cornel West states: "The American Dream is individualistic. King's dream was collective. The American Dream says, "I can engage in upward mobility and live the good life." King's dream was fundamentally Christian. His commitment to radical love had everything to do with his commitment to Jesus of Nazareth, and his dream had everything to do with community, with a "we" consciousness that included poor and working people around the world, not just black people."[1]

This pretty much sums up Dr. King's and many, if not most Progressive Black clergy in America's view of Christianity and redemption. Their view is that the Bible and faiths of the Bible call for a collective redemption and salvation. Whereas orthodox Christianity calls individuals to repent and seek personal salvation through the blood of Christ. This collective salvation hinges on what the group does for all, vs. what the individual does. In other words, people are judged by the various group(s) they belong to and how the collective acts, as redemption is a collective event. Therefore, if a race is oppressor or oppressed, the entire race is judged by the actions of the few. This is why today we see the White race, masculine gender, wealthy class, heterosexual masses, and other groups as inherently evil, while all of those outside of those groups are victims. Therefore, we hear terms like, "White privilege," and the "One Percent," etc.

Another thing most people have forgotten and in some cases even buried, is regarding his popularity and significance. We now honor him with a holiday and speak about his immense contributions to the cause of civil rights. While he was initially a voice, if not the voice, of civil rights, his was not the only influential voice leading to civil rights movement.

For those who have forgotten and those who are too young to remember Dr. King's iconic "I Have A Dream" speech was given at the March on Washington in 1963. I recall, as a 12 year old, watching this speech, live from my uncle and aunt's home in North Philadelphia where I was living at the time. The "March on Washington" was an incredible event and Dr. King's speech was one of the greatest ever given. As powerful and inspirational as the speech was, however, Dr. King's popularity among Black Americans soon waned under criticism by Malcolm X, H. Rap Brown, Stokely Carmichael and others, who did not hesitate to consider and label Dr. King an "Uncle Tom." I still remember in 1964, a year after the March on Washington, my father telling me Dr. King was in trouble and had lost his influence as a voice of and to the Black community. While he was not a radical but a career soldier, my father liked to watch and listen to Stokely and H. Rap. You may wonder then how Dr. King rose to become such an iconic figure warranting a national holiday, monument and much more.

In March of 1965 Dr. King came out for the first time as anti-Vietnam War. In August of that year he stated on CBS's "Face The Nation" program, it was his prophetic role as one who stands for peace, and for the survival of this world, that compels him to take a stand

117

against the war. His opposition to the Vietnam War continued to grow as heard from a sermon given in his home church in Atlanta in January of 1966. While his popularity among Black Americans diminished his opposition to the war grew, so did his popularity among America's "Left." It was this antiwar activity which brought him new influence. Where Dr. King's focus had once been centered on civil rights, his new focus was on "Leftist" and "Progressive" issues. Things ramped up in 1967 when King gave antiwar speeches in LA and Chicago followed by another in New York City. As the antiwar movement grew, so did King's antiwar voice, as well as his popularity. It was not all positive as the NAACP and some black leaders questioned his linking the antiwar issue to civil rights. By this time though, Dr. King was fully invested in this movement.

While influences and interests early on steered him mainly toward the civil rights movement, Dr. King also had an interest in the Labor Movement. While American "Labor" was white controlled and not interested in the "plight" of black Americans, internationally socialists and communists had long been trying to make inroads into that community. They saw Black America as their real hope in achieving the overthrow of America's Capitalist system. As early as 1961, Dr. King gave a keynote speech at the AFLCIO annual convention. In that speech he spoke against "Right to Work" laws, which allowed workers to choose whether or not to join a union. Most of us forget why Dr. King was in Memphis, where he was shot and gave his also famous "I HAVE BEEN TO THE MOUNTAIN TOP speech, shortly before his assassination. It was not for any civil rights event or action, per se; it was in support of a labor strike by black, Memphis, sanitation workers and their AFSCME (American Federation of State, County and Municipal Employees) union.

To his credit, Dr. King always held the civil rights of black Americans as his primary goal, however, I am convinced he saw an alignment with the labor movement in America as a means to that goal. Dr. King, while making grand speeches and interlacing them with talk of the almighty and Jesus, in reality put his real hope and faith in the Labor and Social Justice movements. The problem was and is that, to this day, the majority of Labor and Social Justice organizations and movements not only have nothing to do with God, but often stand against faith and belief in a supernatural entity, particularly THE Super Natural entity.

Dr. King chose to align himself with people who not only had no interest in faith (particularly the Christian faith) but who in many cases stood diametrically opposed to it. Rather than aligning with Black predecessors such as Frederick Douglas and Booker T. Washington who deeply relied upon their faith in God, Dr. King aligned with W.E.B. DuBois who relied upon intellect and the power and influence of men and intellect vs. the power of God. Both DuBois and King lived out the scripture, 2 Timothy 3:5a, "Having the appearance of godliness but denying the power thereof."

In 1950 Dr. King wrote an Autobiographical Paper. In it he stated the following:

"Now for a more specific phase of my religious development. It was at the age of five that I joined the church. I well remember how this event occurred. Our church was in the midst of the spring revival, and a guest evangelist had come down from Virginia. On Sunday morning the guest evangelist came into our Sunday School to talk to us about salvation, and after a short talk on this point, he extended an invitation to any of us who wanted to join the church. My sister was the first one to join the church that morning, and after seeing her join I decided that I would not let her get ahead of me, so I was the next. I had never given this matter a thought, and **even at the time of [my] baptism I was unaware of what was taking place. From this it seems quite clear that I joined the church not out of any dynamic conviction, but out of a childhood desire to keep up with my sister."**

He continues... "Conversion for me was never an abrupt something. **I have never experienced the so-called "crisis moment." Religion has just been something that I grew up in.** Conversion for me has been the gradual intaking of the noble ideals set forth in my family and my environment, and I must admit that this intaking has been largely unconscious. The church has always been a second home for me. As far back as I can remember I was in church every Sunday. I guess this was inevitable since my father was the pastor of my church, yet I never regretted going to church until I passed through a state of skepticism in my second year of college. My best friends were in Sunday School, and it was the Sunday School that helped me to build the capacity for getting along with people.

The lessons which I was taught in Sunday School were in the fundamentalist line. None of my teachers ever doubted the infallibility of the Scriptures. Most of them were unlettered and had never heard of Biblical criticism. Naturally, I accepted the teachings as they were being given to me. I never felt any need to doubt them, at least at that time I didn't. **I guess I accepted Biblical studies uncritically until I was about twelve years old. But this uncritical attitude could not last long, for it was contrary to the very nature of my being.** I had always been the questioning and precocious type. At the age of 13 **I shocked my Sunday School class by denying the bodily resurrection of Jesus.** From the age of thirteen and on, doubts began to spring forth unrelentingly. At the age of fifteen I entered college and more and more could I see a gap between what I had learned in Sunday School and what I was learning in college. This conflict continued until I studied a course in Bible in which **I came to see that behind the legends and myths of the Book** were many profound truths which one could not escape." [2]

In Seminary King wrote a paper titled: "**What Experiences of Christians Living in the Early Christian Century Led to the Christian Doctrines of the Divine Sonship of Jesus, the Virgin Birth, and the Bodily Resurrection.**" [2]

In this paper Dr. King deals with three central themes of the Christian faith. 1) His divinity, 2) His virgin birth, and 3) His bodily resurrection. I do not think I need to tell you these are at the core of orthodox Christian belief. Without any of these three, Jesus is reduced to not only a mere mortal but to a liar or a lunatic.

In this paper King states the following:

"But if we delve into the deeper meaning of these doctrines, and somehow strip them of their literal interpretation, we will find that they are based on a profound foundation. Although we may be able to argue with all degrees of logic that these doctrines are historically and philosophically untenable, yet we can never undermine the foundation on which they are based. The first doctrine of our discussion which deals with the divine sonship of Jesus went through a great process of development. It seems quite evident that the early followers of Jesus in Palestine were well aware of his genuine humanity.

We may find a partial clue to the actual rise of this doctrine (his divinity), in the spreading of Christianity into the Greco-Roman world. I need not elaborate on the fact that the Greeks were very philosophical minded people. Through philosophical thinking the Greeks came to the point of subordinating, distrusting, and even minimizing anything physical. Anything that possessed flesh was always undermined in Greek thought. And **so in order to receive inspiration from Jesus the Greeks had to apotheosize him.**

What Jesus brought into life was a new personality and those who came under its spell were more and more convinced that he with whom they had walked and talked in Galilee could be nothing less than a divine person. To the earliest Christians this breath-taking conviction was not the conclusion of an argument, but the inescapable solution of a problem. Who was this Jesus? They saw that Jesus could not merely be explained in terms of the psychological mood of the age in which he lived, for such explanation failed to answer another inescapable question: Why did Jesus differ from many others in the same setting? And so, the early Christians answered this question by saying that he was the divine son of God.

The second doctrine in our discussion posits the virgin birth. This doctrine gives the modern scientific mind much more trouble than the first, for it seems downright improbable and even impossible for anyone to be born without a human father. First, **we must admit that the evidence for the tenability of this**

121

doctrine is too shallow to convince any objective thinker. *To begin with, the earliest written documents in the New Testament make no mention of the virgin birth. Moreover, the Gospel of Mark, the most primitive and authentic of the four, gives not the slightest suggestion of the virgin birth. The effort to justify this doctrine on the grounds that it was predicted by the prophet Isaiah is immediately eliminated, for all New Testament scholars agree that the word virgin is not found in the Hebrew original, but only in the Greek text which is a mistranslation of the Hebrew word for "young woman."*

The last doctrine in our discussion deals with the resurrection story. This doctrine, upon which the Easter Faith rests, symbolizes the ultimate Christian conviction: that Christ conquered death. From a literary, historical, and philosophical point of view this doctrine raises many questions. **In fact, the external evidence for the authenticity of this doctrine is found wanting.**[4]

I did not make this up, from these words and writings alone (there are many more) we see that Dr. King was not a believer in the orthodox Christian beliefs, that Jesus was Divine, born of a Virgin or Resurrected. Dr. King, like so many religious leaders today professed a Christian faith but denied the core tenants of that faith. They like the message but not the power behind the messenger. Like some today who call themselves "Red Letter Christians," (in many bibles Jesus' words are printed in red), do not accept some, if not much, that does not fit their secular humanist belief system. As Paul wrote in 2 Timothy 3:5 they are: **"Having a form of godliness, but denying the power thereof..."**

This creates or should create a real problem for those who believe in the authority of the scriptures, an authority that comes from the authority of God and His son Jesus. Let me repeat that I, like many, believe Dr. King was a great personality and did much good in bringing the racial issues of America to the forefront. I also, however, want to keep things in balance, not assigning spiritual value to someone or something that has none. I do not hold Dr. King and his worldview any higher than I do that of Malik Shabazz aka, Malcom X. A critical study of the writings and speeches of Malcom X will show, his thoughts and views may actually have been more insightful than those of Dr. King.

I find it interesting that, while Dr. King essentially claimed Jesus' life and message had been mythologized, his own life and story have risen to almost a mythological stature.

As I stated at the beginning of the discussion of Dr. King, his personal life was just that, his personal life, and as a man myself, seeing what is in men (and women) can understand personal failings or shortcomings. I hold none of that, true or false, against Dr. King. I do, however, feel it important to express where I believe he could and should have done more for the true advancement of the descendants of slaves. I feel his message was co-opted and, therefore, failed to achieve a real or significant change in the status of the race. While we see certain segments and individuals within the Black community having success and influence, the masses of descendants of African slaves languish in poverty, crime and have no real direction. As I have discussed, many of these have become "pets" of the "White Liberal Establishment." This is surely not the dream Dr. King spoke of in his 1963 speech. Rather, it has become a nightmare and many, if not most, do not even recall the core message of that speech. That message was one of unity and of a colorblindness. I seriously doubt what Dr. King saw from that "Mountain Top," was the immense poverty, the millions relying on government programs, the failing inner city schools, the alarming number of aborted black babies, the epidemic proportion of killings or the overall seeming helplessness of so many in the Black Community.

Sadly, we have become more and more color conscious, less free and more bitter the farther we have gotten away from the essence of the "Dream." There is only one hope to restore that dream. That is a return to the God of the bible and His message.

Disciples of MLK

Following the assassination of Dr. King there rose a new generation of Black leaders. Among them the most prominent were [and are] the Reverends Jesse Jackson and Al Sharpton. Jesse Jackson's Operation Push and Al Sharpton's National Action Network have been influential in the Black community. While Jesse Jackson began on a more conservative and positive note with his "I Am Somebody" slogan and campaign, his message eventually devolved into a "I am nobody, what can you do for me" situation.

Today you hear various Conservatives say, "If only MLK were still with us, he would be a conservative and a Republican. He was not like them." I beg to differ. MLK, like DuBois was just like them and merely a precursor to the leaders of today. There is no reason to believe Dr. King would hold any different positions from Rev. Jackson or Rev Sharpton.

Jesse Jackson, Al Sharpton, Dr. King and Du Boise relied on the benevolence of their white associations. DuBois was neither the founder nor the head of the NAACP. He was an employee and worked, wrote, and spoke on behalf of his white benefactors, including the eugenicist and founder of Planned Parenthood, Margaret Sanger. It is not known how or from what source(s) Dr. King received an income BUT considering he gave away $54,000 from winning the Nobel Peace Prize, it appears he did not need it. He, nevertheless, managed, somehow, to make a living which included lots of travel and stays in hotels. Please do not get me wrong, I am not opposed to people getting paid for their work, and that includes pastors and preachers. I just feel it is good to know where those funds are coming from and what influence those funds might bring to bear upon the recipient. It is interesting to me that we are always hearing of Christian pastors, of "megachurches," being questioned about their finances, yet no one seems to ask or care from where people like those mentioned above received their incomes.

This root of bitterness turned into hatred rots the soul and destroys a person from the inside out. As is the case with so much of Black America today, this bitterness has crippled 70% or more of the Black community rendering millions of potentially gifted individuals powerless to navigate and succeed in life or to help others do so.

Chapter 16

ANGEL OF LIGHT AND BLACK DEVILS

I do not believe any race is inherently more evil, more superior or more inferior to another. As the Apostle Paul said, "ALL HAVE SINNED and ALL HAVE COME SHORT OF THE GLORY OF GOD." *Rom. 3:23.* Having said that, I also believe there are evil people in all races and given the opportunity these people have the power to enact major damage.

We often hear about Roman Emperor Nero, Adolf Hitler, Joseph Stalin, Pol Pot, and others. Few can dispute these were evil men. Unfortunately, we fail to hear about other, more modern evil doers and what they have done and continue to do.

There is one such person who has, in my opinion, committed a great evil, yet has been and continues to be heralded as a heroine by many today. That person is Margaret Sanger. Many know the name and know what she is known for. Margaret Sanger was a champion of woman's reproductive, or I prefer, nonproductive rights, and the founder of what is known today as Planned Parenthood.

Planned Parenthood has been and remains thought of by many as a place for counselling on family planning. Recently they have shifted into presenting themselves as a "woman's health" organization or medical provider. I remember first hearing of Planned Parenthood in the 60s and thinking of it as a place where young couples can go and get help in planning their future. Well, no, that is not it. Planned Parenthood should more appropriately be called "Unplanned Parenthood." Initially when abortions were illegal, they helped in recommending and dispensing birth control. However, as abortion became legal, Planned Parenthood became the leading provider of abortions and abortion counseling. If you did not plan on having a baby, you would go to Planned Parenthood and they would help you terminate the pregnancy, by either providing the service inhouse or telling you where you could go to receive an abortion. While they do provide some examinations and counseling, do not be fooled, abortion is their number one business.

Why do I bring up Planned Parenthood in this book? The overwhelming number of abortions, per capita, in America, are performed on Black women.

To get an idea of Planned Parenthood and their foundational ideology, we have to go back to its founder, Margaret Sanger. Planned Parenthood describes Sanger as follows: "Our founder, Margaret Sanger, was **a woman of heroic accomplishments, yet like all heroes she was also complex and imperfect.**"

In 1914 Sanger published her own paper called "The Woman Rebel." The title of the first edition said it all: "The Woman Rebel." The masthead slogan was titled **"No gods. No Masters."** In this periodical she gave contraceptive advice. In August of the same year, she was arrested and indicted for obscenity (providing sexual and contraceptive advice) inciting murder and defending assassination. Sanger defended the assassination of "tyrants" including American figures. To avoid 45 years of imprisonment (if found guilty) Sanger fled to Canada and from Canada to England. She returned to the states after a year and founded a clinic. For this she was arrested and spent 30 days in prison. As is so often the case, her time in prison made her a national celebrity generating a great deal of financial support from around the country. Women movements, women's rights and women's suffrage spurred Margaret Sanger's birth control movement as well.

Another issue Sanger championed was the "overpopulation" of the world. Sanger used and combined the ideas of women's liberation, fear of overpopulation, and eugenics (only the fittest survive) to advocate for birth control and eventually abortion. One of the problems facing Planned Parenthood in defending Sanger is the idea of what is "fit and unfit." She believed not everyone should be allowed to have children and those who do should be limited on how many they can have. In short she supported Eugenics, the control of who should be allowed to give birth and how many children should be born.

Many conservatives believe Sanger was a racist and point to her speaking before the KKK at their rallies. I do not take that position. I believe Sanger, like myself, did not believe in a distinction of race as being defined by color. To Margaret Sanger there were just two categories, the fit and the unfit. Like so many Liberals or Progressives,

Sanger had no more love for poor, ignorant whites than she did for any other color or ethnicity. In fact, in support of forced sterilization of those deemed physically and mentally challenged she wrote:

"I admire the courage of a government that takes a stand on sterilization of the unfit and second, my admiration is subject to the interpretation of the word 'unfit.' If by 'unfit' is meant the physical or mental defects of a human being, that is an admirable gesture, but if 'unfit' refers to races or religions, then that is another matter which I frankly deplore."

Margaret Sanger Papers Project
The "Feeble-Minded" and the "Fit":
What Sanger Meant When She Talked about Dysgenics
13, Tuesday Dec. 2016

Here we see Sanger, like so many of today's Progressives, was not as concerned about race as she was about, in her mind, physical and mental standing. Again, Sanger I believe, like myself, did not see race as an issue, it was human mental and material fitness that drove her. To that end she would speak to any group, particularly groups dealing with higher risk of lesser traits. She spoke to the National Urban League (working with inner city Black communities, AND the Ku Klux Klan (rural poor and ignorant whites), in the same year.

As Black communities tended to be poor and more prone to having at risk qualities among their population, Sanger felt a need to focus her attention there. To that end she enlisted so-called educated and upwardly mobile Blacks to introduce what she called "The Negro Project."

Eugenics became favored by many black intellectuals most notably W.E.B. DuBois, Mary McCleod Bethune and Charles S. Johnson, the first Black president of Fisk College, Kelly Miller, Dean of the College of Arts and Science at Howard University, Rev. Adam Clayton Powell Sr. and many others. These people, who are all revered as "Black heroes" today, supported Sangers's "Negro Project." They were Black intellectuals and Eugenicists. They supported culling the "Black Herd."

This was the so-called "Black Intelligentsia", or the cream of DuBois' "Talented Tenth," not the KKK or Margaret Sanger alone supporting this idea.

In 1917, Dr. Kelly Miller penned an article using a Howard University research project titled, "Eugenics Of The Negro Race."[1] In it using so-called research from Howard professors and graduates, he stated a threat of "Race Suicide." His issue was not an attack on the Black race from without, his concern was with the destruction of the Black race from within. This thinking was easy to deduce from "The Talented Tenth." While DuBois spoke of the gifted and talented top 10% of the race leading us out of poverty and ignorance, it did not take a PhD degree to figure out his thinking would lead to a class struggle, with the upper class despising the lower class and vice versa. Miller wrote: **"The upper class is headed towards extinction unless reinforced FROM the fruitful mass below."** Not BY the fruitful mass but rather FROM. In other words, in layman's terms, we must do something because these ignorant Negros are reproducing faster than the rest of us, the elite. This must be stopped.

In the article, "A Question of Negro Health," Charles S. Johnson wrote, **"Eugenic discrimination" was necessary for the Negro.**[2] In *The Birth Control Review*, June 1932, pages 167-169,[2] he spoke of high maternal and infant mortality rates, along with diseases and the difficulty in large families sustaining themselves.

Du Bois expressed his views when he wrote: **"...the Negro must learn that among human races and groups, as among vegetables, quality and not mere quantity really counts."** He also wrote, "the more intelligent class exercised birth control, and the increase among Negroes, even more than the increase among whites, is from that part of the population least intelligent and fit, and least able to rear their children properly."[1] These are just a few of the people and views that supported and were supported by Margaret Sanger from within the Black community.

Then there is this, Sanger's most damning statement, which is hard to justify despite the efforts of Planned Parenthood, which is her statement on the reason for the Negro Project. In a December 1939 letter to the black minister, Clarence Gamble, Sanger said the following regarding the "Negro project."

> *"We do not want word to go out that we want to exterminate the Negro population and the minister is the man who can straighten out that idea, if it ever occurs to any of their more rebellious members."*

Margaret Sanger was not a racist, as many of my Conservative peers want us to believe. She was the epitome of the real struggle. As I keep trying to convey, it is not a struggle of race, **it is a struggle of the elite (in their eyes) vs. the common.** Margaret Sanger, like the elitist Progressives of today, despised everyone they deemed inferior.

Black elitists are among the worst. Growing up in both upper and lower class Black neighborhoods as well as very integrated ones, I can tell you first hand the things elitist blacks say about their "inferior" or as DuBois put it "unfit" brethren. It makes anything whites say derogatorily about Black people seem like nothing. The fear of and loathing for their "inferior" people is shocking. This attitude is found mostly among the pseudo intellectual Black elite class; your educators and professional class. They have convinced themselves that they are a special class among themselves; they are actually schizophrenic. On the one hand they want to claim all of the privileges of "Blackness" and that heritage, while living in a culturally white world, rejecting those who remain in the depressed urban communities. This allows them to blame "Whitey", while not doing anything substantive to better the plight of their fellow Black folks. In fact, the worse it is for the common Black person, the better they feel about themselves for being better than them. Yet, it is "Whitey's" fault.

To be fair to Margaret Sanger and her posterity in Planned Parenthood, I do not consider her as an enemy of the Black Community. She and her posterity are an enemy to all humanity. From promoting contraception, to legalizing abortion, and eventually, if allowed to continue, euthanasia, her believers will go against everything that makes humans human. It will truly be the Darwinian "survival of the fittest" contest. There will be an integrated society ethnically, but the real attempt will be to cut off those deemed unfit, and those who hold back the rest. I have one question for those who accept this thinking? Where do you draw the line? Where does the fit/unfit line begin and end? I believe it will be an ever moving and always upward line. There will always be someone deemed unfit or less fit. This is the human condition, the sinfulness of selfishness and greed. You cannot eradicate that with selective breeding or non-breeding, as Nazi, Germany proved.

Since abortion was legalized in 1973, there have been over 63 million aborted children. Think about that. Think of the nations in this world that do not have 63 million people. Initially Black abortions comprised about 1/4th of all abortions, which is already a high proportion, but that number has increased to where Black abortions now lead all others with 50% of all women seeking abortions being Black. What makes that figure more disturbing is that, while Black abortions are at or over 50% of all abortions, the Black population only comprises 12.5% of all ethnicities. Meanwhile, the White population comprises over 70% of the United States. Therefore, Black abortions are not only half of all abortions, they are 5 times the rate of white abortions. As a result, where Black Americans were the 2nd largest ethnic group in the country 10 years ago, we are now number three having been passed by Hispanics who are approaching 19%.

As a believer in a personal God and that His will is represented by His word (the Bible), it is my basic belief that life begins at conception. While it is a process, it is a fact that LIFE is created once the single sperm wins the race, hits the egg and the first cell division begins. While I understand the frustration with seeing people or certain segments of society in poverty, uneducated, often ill, prone to crime and delinquency, etc., the answer is not to end life before it begins. You do not make someone's life better by ending another life. If we followed that logic to its logical conclusion, there would be no end to killing, as there is always someone to blame for failing. The answer is not to end life but to work to make everyone's life better. DuBois was partially right when he said it was not about quantity rather quality of life, BUT his definition of quality was to limit those who would have that quality by limiting the quantity, instead of working to help the less fortunate. That will ALWAYS, inevitably lead to a never-ending, redefining of what quality is and who gets to enjoy it. I am sure Hitler, Pol Pot, Marx, Lenin, Stalin, and Mao all had some notion they were doing it for the good of the fit. Unfortunately, it did not end well for the less fortunate, or for themselves, in the end.

Chapter 17

WHITE PRIVILEGE / WHITE GUILT

O ne thing not helpful to the social, educational and economic maturing of those we identify as "People Of Color," is the promotion of the ideas of "White Privilege" and "White Guilt." Not only are these presented as a legitimate cause of non-white failure, many have turned selling these ideas into a business. These ideas and their direct cousin "Victimhood" are, in my opinion, more responsible for non-white failures than anything the KKK, slavery, Jim Crow or any other entity could have accomplished. The reason I believe these are dangerous and deadly is that they justify and nourish victimhood. It establishes and promotes what President George W. Bush called **"The soft bigotry of low expectations."**

The idea of "White Guilt" and "White Privilege" are a byproduct of years of blame and shame heaped upon Europeans and their descendants for the plight of non-whites worldwide. "White Guilt" is not confined to America, but like a pandemic it has spread throughout the "Free World." I say "Free World," because nations under socialist and communist rule do not only seem free from this sickness but have been given a free pass. This, despite the fact these nations have lower non-white populations than the U.S. and many western European nations, have more restrictive immigration laws and greater discrimination, thus being clearly opposed to non-white success.

In fact, the freer and the more accommodating the nation, the more it seems to be constantly accused of being racist and purposely holding back its non-white residents. The three nations which have the most protests and riots by or about people of color are the U.S., England, and France. These countries are considered anti-Black, and anti-foreigner, as well as anti any person or group seeking special privilege.

One of the more puzzling things I have found is among the biggest champions of the "White Privilege" message are whites. Organizations like The Southern Poverty Law Center and individuals like Rachel Dolezal (aka **Nkechi Amare Diallo)**, Tim Wise (and others) have managed to enshrine this idea in modern American culture, from our educational system to the corporate level.

At the same time, they have elevated themselves financially and status wise, selling the idea of "White Privilege." Take for example Rachel Dolezal a blond, white woman who made herself up to look the part of a black, radical, woman; a "Soul Sister." She pretended to be black, became a "Black Activist" and head of a chapter of the NAACP until she was exposed as a total fraud.

There is Shawn King, self-proclaimed leader and founder of "Black Lives Matter," until it was exposed that he is neither. Like Dolezal, he has consistently faced questions, if he is really Black.

Then there is Timothy Wise. His is an interesting situation. Wise (of European and half Jewish heritage) never pretended to be black but has made a career of speaking and writing on "White Privilege." I guess the "Abused Jew" lobby was overcrowded so he got on the "White Privilege" and "You poor Black folks" train. Some of his best known titles include: *White Like Me: Reflections on Race From a Privileged Son; Affirmative Action: Racial Preference in Black and White; Speaking Treason Fluently: Anti-Racist Reflections From an Angry White Male;* and *White Lies Matter: Race, Crime, and the Politics of Fear in America.*

Wise has been a popular speaker at hundreds of universities and has been tapped as a consultant to corporations and law enforcement on race issues. In fact, Wise has made a pretty nice career of telling black people how privileged he and other whites are by just being white. His booking site reads:

> *"If Tim Wise's booking fee is outside your companies (sic) budget or your (sic) unable to align with his appearance availability, our booking agents can provide you a list of talent that aligns with your event theme, budget and event date."[1]*

In other words, you may not be able to afford this gifted white guy, but we have others that may be affordable at a discount. I guess his fee is an example of his white privilege which has allowed him to make a living from talking about that privilege. Ironically, these people, and others have achieved fame and influence not from being white but by convincing Black people, white privilege is a thing. Strangely, each of them would be nobodies if they did not get their "bonafides" from Black folks. Is it not strange, but comical to an extent, that you have white people making their living off of Black people, convincing them white people are privileged? That would be like me convincing Asians or Native Americans to pay me to tell them how privileged I am by not being Asian or Native American. How far do you think that would fly?

What is the idea of "White Privilege?" It is the idea that there is some intrinsic value to being born Caucasian which gives one a head-start and an ongoing advantage in life. In other words, if you take two children born under the same set of circumstances, the white one is provided with an unfair advantage over the non-white one. Of course, this is rarely the case. In reality we are talking about apples and oranges. Of course, a white child born to a family in the middle or upper class is going to have an advantage over a black child born in an urban ghetto, but, that same white child has the same advantage over another WHITE child born in rural, depressed America. Therefore, it is as I have stated before, more about class than color, which makes the difference.

I am not as bothered by people like Dolezal and Wise as I am about Black folks who take them seriously. They are merely smooth-talking con-artists. Here is an example of something Tim Wise wrote about his nemesis, conservative writer and speaker Dinesh D'Souza. For those who are not aware, D'Souza is a dark skinned man of East Indian birth and heritage who according to "White Privilege" proponents should be a victim. Here is how Timothy Wise, the privileged white guy, describes him.

"I'm sure this will come as a shock to no one who has been awake during the past twenty years. But turns out, Dinesh D'Souza — my old nemesis and a man of color is married to a woman named Dixie (I kid you not, this is for real, and it matters)".[2]

Seriously, you are attacking D'Souza for being married to a woman, named Dixie? What is implied in the statement "a man of color, who is married to a woman named Dixie - and it matters," is that Dixie is white and has a racist name. This means D'Souza, regardless of his skin tone or heritage, is also a racist or race traitor at best. Wow!! Here the great champion of Black outrage is implying, a "man of color" who marries outside his race is the opposite of the old term "Nigger lover." I guess he'd like to call him (D'Souza) a "Honky Lover."

Realty Check: There is no such thing as "White Privilege", unless you consider Tim Wise and other White, Liberal Progressives who feel comfortable enough to attack any Black or dark skinned person (D'Souza is DARK and of East Indian background), and people like myself without any repercussion, "privileged".

As I tried to state elsewhere, a few times, race is merely a social construct and an identifier. Before we had non-whites living among whites, and vice versa, the identifiers were dress, vernacular, where one lived, worked, ate, went to school, etc. Everyone knew where the poor and the rich parts of town were. The rich were not allowed to mingle with the poor and vice versa. I love the way the British used to say it. Speaking down to the poor they would speak of being the poor's "Betters." If you have never seen the BBC production "Poldark", you should watch it. It and many other such period pieces give a clear and accurate picture of what life was like before race was introduced to the mix in England and Europe. It was not pretty. "Poldark" does not even begin to scratch the surface of the treatment of the poor in Europe prior to American Independence.

I grew up as a military dependent, an "Army Brat." My father was an enlisted man as opposed to an officer and we had unspoken rules that we did not date or mix with officer's kids. Particularly enlisted men's sons and officer's daughters. It was less risky for a black, enlisted man's kid to date a white enlisted man's daughter, than it was for a white enlisted man's son to date an officer's daughter.

Just recently I learned the vacation spot of the "rich and famous," Martha's Vineyard is segregated, even to this day. There is a black part and a white part to the "Vineyard." The interesting thing about this is black residents of the island are no more hospitable to the lower class black person than the white residents are to the average white person. It is all about class and status. A few years ago, when President Obama and his family were going to vacation there for the first time, there was a big question as to whether the Obama's would vacation on the Black side or the White side of the island. They, of course, chose the white side. Was this a racist choice? No, in no way should it have been seen that way, it was a choice of status. While the black residents were of an elevated status, the rich white folks were more elevated and loftier in the social hierarchy - more and older money. Furthermore, the Black residents of the Vineyard would no more approve of their children mingling with, much more marrying outside of their class than the white residents would allow their children to intermingle with less "fortunate" whites.

I remember watching an infomercial several years ago for "Feed The Children." It was about children living in poverty in the Appalachian Mountains. These were very rural and very poor communities. They were also all white communities. I remember the narrator saying, "you have heard that 1 in 4 children in America go to bed hungry every night. What you have not been told is that 3 out of 4 of those children are white." I was shocked. I like most of us, were wrongly, (thanks to the constant portrayal as such in the media) under the assumption that poverty was confined to black and brown communities. Where is "white privilege" for those children? What advantage do they have? What is their excuse for being poor? Clearly not their skin color.

This brings me to the flip side of this theme and the whole point of, "White Guilt." White guilt has spread in America and much of the world like a pandemic. White people have bought into the notion that the ills of the non-white world are their fault. Not only should they feel guilty about current "White Privilege" but they should feel guilty about the historic privilege (they had) which held back the non-white world. Never mind white advances in science, medicine, business, education, and every other area. To believers in White Guilt, these accomplishments are nothing compared to the devastation caused by White Privilege. We are to believe that non-white civilizations would have been better off had the white man never trodden on their lands. In America, the native population would be better off had Europeans never shown up? Africa would be a better place had the white man never shown up. Do you really believe that?

As a believer in the God of the Bible, I see things very differently. As the late Bahamian pastor and teacher Miles Munroe said, to mixed audiences: "I thank God my ancestors were brought from Africa as slaves." He went on to say that had those ancestors not been brought here, he would not have been able to bring them the gospel in a free and prosperous land. Miles saw what Joseph saw in his enslavement. Miles saw that it equipped him to help and hopefully save many people.

"White guilt" is a fake guilt. It is a clever device to allow some to get "off the hook" and some to personally profit from blaming others. It goes something like this: "I can tell people how bad my ancestors were and how bad other white people are, yet allow myself to enjoy what I have, because I feel your pain. I can make all of the money I can and want, live in what area(s) I want and be guilt free, because I "understand" and "feel" for you poor oppressed people."

At the same time, it creates a fake compassion and does not help those who need to be lifted up. Like the "White Angels" mentioned earlier under" White Privilege," there are "White Angels" making a living selling White Guilt. One such is Robin D'Angelo. Robin had the #1 selling book on Amazon recently. The name of the book is, *"White Fragility: Why It's So Hard for White People to Talk About Racism"*. Additionally, Robin receives a handsome fee for convincing white people they are racist and explaining how they can free themselves from it. Actually, it is merely telling yourself you are a dirtbag, admitting it to others, and voila you are all good.

Another is Jennifer Harvey, the Rev. Dr. Jennifer Harvey to be exact, another enlightened white woman, teaching white people about their guilt and what to do about it. She has several books on the subject of racism, particularly on how to indoctrinate, or excuse me, teach your children about race and racism. Among her titles are, "Raising White Kids: Bringing Up Children in a Racially Unjust America", "Whiteness and Morality: Pursuing Racial Justice through *Reparations and Sovereignty"*, and *"Disrupting White Supremacy: White People on What We Need To Do"*, which she co-edited.

In an NPR interview, June 4, 2020, Dr. Harvey said:

"My daughter is told, 'Police are safe — go find one if you're in trouble,' but her African American cousin is learning complicated messages about the police from his parents. Those differing messages mean they can be great friends for a while. But eventually, the depth of their friendship will erode because my white child will not be able to identify with her African American cousin or her African American friends. White Americans have to teach our kids how to identify with that experience and how to be good friends to black and brown youth as they grow up. That requires us teaching them about racism. And it requires us modeling anti-racism, which is something a lot of white Americans really struggle with."

What utter nonsense, actually filthy garbage, that is. Her white daughter will not be able to be friends with her Black cousin because she "will not be able to identify with her African American cousin and African American friends"? So, you are telling me the "Guru" of how to not raise racist children will fail to prevent her daughter from becoming a racist? Excuse me while I step out and have a hard laugh.

OK I'm back. Here we have a WHITE lady, I think she is a woman, I do not want to gender identify her, that makes a living on teaching others how not to raise racist children, telling us her daughter will grow up to become a racist. If I had bought one of her books or paid to hear her speak, I think I would ask for a refund. I am sure that she, like Jennifer Harvey and the others mentioned above, would say that is how deep and pernicious this racism is. We cannot even control it in ourselves or our children. I think Jesus had a response to this. Before you try and heal someone else, "heal thy self."

My wife and I currently have 4 children and 4 grandchildren. My children are Quadroon. That means 1/4th Black. They spent their early years growing up in Holland and Germany. It does not get much whiter than those two countries, or it did not back then. Never ever did they come home and tell me their friends rejected them because they had Black blood or their father was Black. Our oldest son still has deep friendships with his running buddies from Germany and has been back to visit them a few times. The bond is still there. We did not talk about

139

race at home because it was NEVER an issue. Our daughter has one daughter that is a beautiful brown. Her sister and cousins, (Octoroons) although they tan very well, look white. They have bi-racial and fully white cousins and there is no way on earth that these cousins would ever not share that bond of love and friendship. We never had "The Talk" and never will. Our children and their children are secure in who they are, and not the color of their skin.

To teach white privilege and white guilt and to foster that on children should be a criminal offense. I am reminded again of President George W. Bush's saying the, **"soft bigotry of low expectations"**.

We taught our children, as my father taught me, that they and they alone will determine how far they can and cannot go. I remember coming home from work one day and having one of my son's meet me at the door. The conversation went as follows: "Dad, before you see my grades and get upset, I made a B in math, but I have to tell you that it was not my fault." I responded, "how is that?" He said, "it was a very hard class." I then asked, "did anyone get an A?" To which he responded, "yes, a few people." To which I responded, "then why are you not one of those people?" I did not need to say any more. He got the message. What I did not tell him or the others, was I finished high school and college with a 2.1 GPA. Very average! A very low average.

My parents were both good students and finished at the top of their class, but, as they were from poor backgrounds that did not see much beyond getting a job as soon as you can, they failed to push me and hold me accountable. It was always a foregone conclusion I would attend university, BUT I was not given a mission or shown a vision. I became complacent and lazy doing only what was needed to get by. I spent my entire senior year of high school partying and going to nightclubs (discos, as they were called back then) on school nights, as well as weekends. It was not until I attended seminary a few years after college, that I knew why I was there and worked at it. I refused to do the same with my kids. Another time we had an ice storm in our city and the streets were icy and slick. My wife received a visit from a neighbor telling her one of my sons had run into her car. When I spoke to our son he said, "it was not my fault, it was the ice and her car was parked in the middle of a curve, I could not help it." To which I responded, "were you the only one to come down the street and around that curve?" He said, "no, I was not." I responded, "but you were the only one to hit her car, right?" In his mind the accident was a result of the ice and the lady parking in a bad spot. All of this was partially true, however, he needed to understand that despite other factors, WE are ultimately responsible to navigate the dangers and pitfalls that confront us. As a result of teaching accountability, I have adult children who are able to make decisions and successfully navigate through life, its dangerouss and pitfalls. They do not wait or look for excuses, they deal with life's challenges, solving problems and figuring things out, without a need to blame others. I also have relatives and friends who are 100% free of "White Guilt". I will never put that on anyone or allow anyone to put that on someone I know or love.

I use these examples to say, "White Guilt" and a victimhood mentality are not helpful in uplifting the downtrodden. Those selling this lie straight from the "Pit of Hell", are ignorant fools or evil deceivers, merchandising to a gullible community. They need to be resisted and openly challenged. They are polluting the minds of Blacks and Whites alike. It is one thing to mislead adults (who should know better), however, when they begin misleading children and young people, I have to say NO, not on my watch. We need more people to say and do the same. Do not allow these charlatans to infect and destroy the minds of a generation. Call them out for what they are, lying deceivers and racial pimps.

Black Americans have gone through a tough time. They were enslaved, beaten, mistreated, persecuted, and belittled. However, others have been as well, here in America, both before and after their arrival. As Booker T. Washington said, "...if any race or person is to truly succeed in this nation, they must pass through the "American Crucible".

As I am writing these words our country is going through the largest, most prolific and longest lasting protests and riots in our nation's history. What is so different about this time is in June 2020 Pew Research and media fact finders reported those who attended a protest focused on racial equality were 48% white, 22% Hispanic, 8% Asian and 17% black. What sparked this national outbreak was the needless killing of a Black man suspected of passing a forged $20 bill. The video evidence appears to show a clear case of police brutality, specifically the actions of one police officer whose brutality resulted in the man's death. The video shows three other officers standing by, allowing it to happen. I know of few, if anyone, who has seen the video evidence fails to see it as a crime. Democrat, Republican, Black, White, you name it, most agree this was unnecessary. The President came out early on and condemned the killing, as did members of federal, state, and local governments of both parties. Even police throughout the nation agree this was a tragedy and a needless death. Yet, instead of peaceful protests, violent protests have emerged, injuring innocent people and destroying innocent property, supposedly in the name of "Social Justice".

As I said, this series of riots appears to not only have white rioters but more white than black rioters. The riots appear to be orchestrated and driven by certain white elements for purposes beyond the so-called "Social Justice" motive. You have white agitators throwing things, starting incidents, attacking law enforcement, and destroying property, followed by black rioters looting. It is an amazing but sad thing to watch.

While all of this is taking place, we see normal citizens excusing the behavior as understandable, or in some cases encouraging it. It is as though the world has lost its collective mind. What would cause people to excuse or encourage such lawless behavior? Back to the original subject at hand, "White Privilege" and "White Guilt" I cannot tell you how many interviews and reports I have seen in which I hear someone say, "We have to understand the frustration of these people. They feel they have no other recourse." Also, "This rioting is a response to the injustice and oppression these people have historically suffered as a result of "systemic racism."

I get particularly upset watching the NFL network, or being told in tweets from Black Millionaires spouting "Social Injustice," how horrible America has been (and continues to be) to Black people. Seriously? 80% of the on-air personnel of those programs are Black and 70% to 80% of athletes in the NFL and NBA are Black. Looking at that you could talk about "athletic injustice". I refer you back to the discussion of the "NEWBOs." I suspect these people are suffering from "Black (Success) Guilt". They got theirs and now feel they need to somehow help those less fortunate. Rather than give up their incomes to build and revitalize their communities, they blame it on and attack others under the guise of "Social Justice." It is someone else's fault and problem but send your kids to their football or basketball camp and things will be good. You've given back to my community? Wow, really?!

To sum this up, let me just say, privilege is not defined by melanin. Guilt falls upon both Blacks and Whites who currently have the power to change their surroundings but do not. There is no future in the past. When Jesus said in Matt. 25:40, "Whatsoever you do," he was really asking, What did YOU do?"

It is not about what white people or anyone else did to Black people or for Black people. It is about what we do, or do not do, to and for each other today. Let's lose the guilt and the notion of privilege and accept that ALL LIVES MATTER. Let's ask: "What can I personally do to better the lives of others.

Chapter 18

HOW THE JEWS SURVIVED AND THRIVED

T he Jews by race and faith have not only survived but rather thrived over the past 4000 or so years since their existence. Theirs is an interesting history.

Most of us forget or are never taught that Jew is not a race. I always find it funny to hear people speak of anti-Semitism as a racial issue. Jews were carved out of the same group as modern day Iraqis and Arabs. Abraham the father of the Jewish nation was himself born in the city of Ur, which still exists and is at the southernmost end of Iraq. He travelled north to Haran, which is located in southern Turkey near the border of Syria. At the age of 75, Abraham left Haran and travelled to the land of Canaan, modern day Israel.

Abraham's entire time in this new land was one of constant adversity. He was essentially the unwelcomed new neighbor from another town. Kind of like a New York Yankee moving to Georgia or Texas or vice versa. To make things worse, this new neighbor was prospering beyond all of the locals, which failed to endear him and his family to the residents of Israel.

It somewhat reminds me of the sharecropper that ends up doing better than his peers and even the one who gave him the land to share in the first place. One such person was Junius G. Groves, born in 1859, a slave in Kentucky, who took part in what was called the Black Exodus or "The Blexodus" after emancipation and the Civil War. Groves came to Edwardsville, KS after a short stop in Kansas City. He did not like segregated city life and preferred the rural life of a farmer. He worked for a white farmer and after a while, saving his earnings and building relationships with other white farmers, he was able to purchase land of his own. His farm grew so prosperous that he became known as the "Potato King of the World," for growing more potatoes than any other farm in the country.

Abraham, the father of Israel, while befriending some of his neighbors, was also at odds with many. He never actually owned any of the land he dwelt upon. The only plot he ever purchased was a family burial plot. There was constant strife with his neighbors and servants and those of his nephew Lot to the point he and Lot parted ways. Abraham spent a somewhat strange and short period in Egypt where he left with not a little booty from the Egyptian king who paid him to leave. Abraham had two sons, the first, Ishmael, from one of his servants, who would become the father of the Arab people and Isaac, who would became the first born of the Jewish nation.

From Abraham, Isaac, Jacob and Jacob's 12 sons we not only get the nation and people called Israel or Jews, but we get some terrible examples of a messed up family. I go back to the song I shared earlier, "Family," with the lyrics, "they might be crazy, but they is my family." Yes, they were messed up but they always remained or came back together.

Throughout history Jews suffered much, yet each time they seem to prosper. From their time in Egypt, Babylon, Persia, dispersed throughout Europe and the world, they somehow rose again together, more successful, more prosperous and more powerful than ever.

Many, if not most, Jews roday do not have a strong genetic connection to Abraham, Isaac or Jacob. So, what makes a Jew, a Jew? It is identifying with the idea of being Jewish. Many people throughout history have converted to Judaism as a faith, then their descendants claimed Jewish heritage. Some, if not many modern Jews, reject the faith of Abraham, Isaac and Jacob, but still claim their "Jewishness", nevertheless. Many were and are, not only atheist but rabidly anti-faith. One finds Jews on every side of religion and politics, upholding their Jewish heritage, whether by blood or conversion.

In Genesis 12, God told Abraham to leave his home country and his kinfolk and enter a new land. He promised if he followed God's leading he would create a great nation from him and would bless him, his family and those who were good to Abraham and his family. The other side of that coin was that God would curse whoever cursed or mistreated Abraham or his family.

Throughout history we have seen examples of this. As messed up as Abraham's kids, grandkids and beyond have been, they nevertheless have seen God's favor. I don't understand it, I just must believe it. There are many who, to their own peril, want to believe it mere coincidence that Jews continue to survive and thrive. I am not numbered among them. I am convinced that promise, the eternal covenant between God and Abraham made in Genesis 12, sealed in Genesis 15 and explained in Genesis 22, is real. The covenant was that Abraham, who was not able to have a son, would not only have a son, but would have more sons and daughters than anyone could count.

What people need to realize today, however, especially Black Americans, is God offers us the opportunity to be partakers in that same covenant. To become that "seed of Abraham," the sons and daughters promised through faith in the One who made the covenant. In Romans 2:29 the Apostle Paul asks and then answers the question; "Who is the real Jew"? Paul said, a person is a Jew who is one inwardly; and circumcision is circumcision of the heart, by the Spirit, not by the written law and outward circumcision of the flesh. Such a person's acceptance is not from other people, but from God.

There are Black Americans who (for no reason I can see) despise the Jews. Why would they do that? Yes, Jews have been prosperous and some of their prosperity came through providing goods and services in Black communities. But that was at a time when no one else would sell to or serve Black folks. There was a time when we were thankful to have a store, a lender, a restaurant that served us as we were getting our footing. When and why did the community become ungrateful and turn on those who helped us through difficult times? Think about it, what has a Jewish person ever done to you or anyone you know? I suspect nothing.

My father was raised in Bay St. Louis, Mississippi. He told me of how he grew up on a street with Jewish and Italian families mixed in with Black families. My father always spoke fondly of the Jewish people he knew, as well as of the Italians. They were all friends and they looked out for one another. When did that change and why? Remember Jews were thought of, especially in the South, as not far above Black people. They were considered "Christ Killers," - as dumb as that is.

Beyond the blessing(s) of being Chosen by God, in a more secular sense, another thing we could learn from Jews is helping and supporting one another. I believe the constant persecution and struggle for survival

147

the Jews have endured over the centuries, has created a bond unlike any other among a community of people. We see a similar bond among Asians, entering the country, although more country specific. At a time when they too were persecuted, they banded together and supported each other's businesses, a bond which remains strong today. We see this bond in the Japanese, Chinese, Korean, Vietnamese, Thai and Cambodian communities, much of which is due to their support of one another. Where we rarely see it, at least not since integration, is among Black Americans.

Black Americans have come a long way but have, at the same time, regressed. We have overcome slavery and Jim Crow, however, along the way we lost our way. We lost our sense of family. We lost it in the sense of the nuclear family, a two parent household and sibling bonds, but we also lost it among the community.

While every other people group has been able to integrate into major American society, while retaining their ethnicity, Black Americans have not been able to do so. This is no one's fault but our own. European Americans can be of European descent yet American, Asian Americans can be of Asian descent and American, Hispanics can be of Hispanic descent and American, yet as Blacks we are almost always forced to choose, are you Black or are you American? It is usually spoken of as "acting White", but it is acting American. If we choose to speak proper American English, get good grades, take a certain job, dress a certain way, listen to a certain music, we are not acting American, we are acting White!! Instead of allowing us to assimilate, while having pride in our heritage, we uphold the heritage over assimilation. Ebonics, sagging pants, a certain walk, certain musical tastes make us "legit." Talk white, dress white, walk white and listen to white music and we are outcasts.

If that is so important, how are Jews, Asians and Hispanics, who speak, dress and dare I say it, ACT WHITE, still able to be considered Asian, Jewish, or Hispanic, etc.? Of late, as spoken by Joe Biden, as Democrat candidate for president, the idea is being fostered upon us that to not vote Democrat voids our standing in the Black Community. This is not only tyranny but a sad and losing proposition, to make person or anyone choose between their ethnicity and their nation. That is not the freedom our forefathers fought and died for, or people from all around the world seek to come to this nation for. It is, in fact, what most coming here flee.

Nevertheless, it is this choice Black America has fostered upon its members. Let us learn from the history of the Jews with whom we have so much in common. Let the adversity make us stronger, unite us, and yet allow us to live with pride as full citizens of the United States of America. The nation that has allowed us to become a healthy prosperous and respected people.

Chapter 19
LESSONS FROM WAKANDA

In memory of Chadwick Boseman, King T'Challa, in film *"Black Panther"*

W hen I heard Marvel Studios was doing a film on the comic book character "Black Panther," written by black writers and with a black Director, my first reaction was, oh man here we go, a modern day, "Blacksploitation" film. I must confess however, I liked "Blacksploitation" films. My favorite was the 1972 film "Super Fly".

One of the high points of that time for me, was a weeklong debate in the Texas Tech student newspaper "The University Daily", between myself and their film critic. He hated the film and I loved it. I would write attacking his critique and he would attack my critique of him. I also attacked his "sacred cow", John Wayne films. It lasted over a week and became morning talk, during the "Spades" and Domino games being played in the "Soul Corner" of the student union.

I was in for the surprise of my life and a real treat when the film Black Panther played. It was one of the most entertaining and well done films I had seen in years. I fully understood why it was the number one movie in the world for months. While the cinematography, acting, and production were amazing, the writing was equally amazing. Props to the Director Ryan Coogler and fellow writer Joe Robert Cole. The film captured the true essence of a great story with common yet valuable themes and moral statements. Where it could have been simply about a Black Super Hero, from a Black Super Tribe, the writers, in my opinion, embedded some phenomenal, universal messages and themes, some of which I fear most viewers missed because the film itself, action wise, was so well done.

Here is the deeper message I got from the film. The people and tribes of Wakanda were blessed and favored by a meteor from space landing there, giving them special gifts, knowledge, and power. The Wakanda's guarded these and used them to build a special civilization, kept hidden

151

from the rest of the world. There is one flaw in the story, if I can knit pick. If Wakanda is hidden from anyone's knowledge and has never been discovered, how were the king and his entourage invited to a world summit in the Captain America film that preceded it? OK that's it, I will move on. Just had to get that out.

In any event to go over the story line, the king sent a scout or spy (the king's brother) to the U.S. (deep 'hood) to observe the people living there. The scout goes to Oakland, CA. Why there of all the places on earth? I have no idea. He becomes radicalized, early 70s Black Panther Party style wanting to attack the "white man." The scout is stopped and killed by the king but has a son who grows up embittered toward America and the "White World," as well as Wakanda's for his father's death. Moving forward, the son is now grown up, has been a super, military commando and knows about Wakanda and his royal blood. He makes his way to Wakanda, challenges the prince who has just been made king, for the throne and plots to get revenge on "Whitey" on a global scale.

Now we are caught up and I will not go any further with the story. If you saw the movie you know how it all turns out. What I want to discuss is what I believe are the deeper, true message(s) of this film (at least for me) and how it should move us.

I saw the film as a tiny African nation called Wakanda, with its people, a simple but gifted people, blessed with a gift from outer space. Instead of sharing this gift they kept it hidden and to themselves. I do not think it was for selfish reasons, rather, possibly, they felt the world might not be ready for the gift. The king's brother was sent to check out the outside world, I imagine seeing how they could help make things better. Instead the brother got distracted and embittered by life and what he experienced in "the hood." Another question I have is where was the son's (Erik Killmonger's) mother? But I digress.

The father's bitterness was transferred to his son (Erik) who apparently made it his life's goal to become a trained U.S. military warrior, and to use what he learned, which seems to have been how to kill people, to exact vengeance upon the King's family and the White World.

Meanwhile back in Wakanda, having wanted to exact vengeance of his own, and being helped to overcome that desire by Captain America and the Avengers, Prince T'Challa, the Black Panther himself, was dealing with the weight of having to lead his nation forward following his father's death. T'Challa, overcoming a challenge to his thrown by a rival tribal leader, now finds himself challenged by a more powerful and sinister force, his cousin Erik from Oakland. The film had all of the normal Marvel Avenger motifs and fight scenes but what stood out to me were the underlying messages that resonate in the real world.

Erik Killmonger epitomized the current prevailing Black thought, that Whitey has been in power long enough and it is time to get revenge and subjugate them through force and violence. Erik Killmonger wanted to use the technology and weapons of Wakanda to essentially blow up the Caucasian world. Sound familiar? Meanwhile, the Wakandans realized they had been given the gifts for good, to help the world, not to destroy it or subject others.

In the final scene, which touched me deeply, the Wakandans used their wealth and technology to build schools and businesses in the same inner-city neighborhood Killmonger and his father had lived and become embittered in. The thought then hit me, Wakanda is real. We have a hidden kingdom with wealth, power and technology right here in the U.S. It is the "Newbos". The New Black Overclass.

If the Newbos were to invest in business, education, and technology in the inner cities, what a difference that would make. Instead of football, basketball, and other athletic camps, what if the black millionaire athletes tithed to building businesses, and provide access to healthy foods? What if instead of giving time, money and PR to Black Lives Matter and talking about "Social Justice", they funded their own inner-city police and security force to act how they deem appropriate. What if they built private schools, technology centers, health clinics, etc.? That would go much further than the constant complaining about how others are not doing enough, and the poor pitiful "us" song and dance we constantly hear. We just got word that my fellow former Texas Tech University "Red Raider," now NFL quarterback Patrick Mahomes, has received a world record contract worth $500 million. I wonder what a tithe of $50 million of that could do in the inner city of Kansas City?

What could LeBron James do for his hometown of Cleveland or his new home in LA with a tithe of the millions he has and will continue to make. Money to the Democrat Party, Black Lives Matter, the National Action Network, or the NAACP and others is not going to improve the inner city neighborhoods. It is going to support Progressive candidates and social engineering ideas that have never and will never work. We have all heard the old definition that insanity is "doing the same thing over and over and expecting a different result." Nothing better fits that definition of insanity than giving money and energy to the same entities which have received funds for decades and not only have failed to improve the communities they claim to help, but rather have watched those communities get worse.

At this point, I must charge the Black Church as well. Think of the millions that have gone into the coffers of churches in inner cities over the past few centuries. How is it they have allowed their communities to decay so? We have pastors and staff members living in nice homes, driving the finest cars and wearing the finest clothes. We give them and their spouses fancy titles such as Bishop, Apostle, Prophet, and First Lady, while so many of their members are looking for hope and direction for a better life. When the church fails to offer that hope in a tangible way, instead delivering "Pie in the Sky" or super spiritual messages, it is natural for people to look for whomever offers what all humans crave, regardless if they can or will ever produce it. I am charging the "Black Church" because these are their people. Unfortunately, instead of meeting the real needs of their people, many black pastors support BLM and a Black Nationalist message because they are afraid of losing their membership to a "White church".

Instead of preaching and teaching on the dignity and responsibility of every individual, their messages are centered around all of the evil men do. Especially pernicious is the message that we are in bad shape because a certain segment of society keeps us there. "WHITEY"!

I find it funny certain pastors consistently preach on the power of God but that same all powerful God is incapable of freeing us from the clutches and power of the white man. The message is, a Republican president and Congress as well as whites in general, are more powerful than God. God can answer your prayers, and do anything, EXCEPT, what Republicans and other white people won't allow Him to do. If that is the case, their god is too weak and not God.

I have to say the Wakandans, while never mentioning religion, did a better job of living out the Gospel than many churches do today. While their gift supposedly came from outer space, (we are never told what planet or source) one could say it was from God. The Wakandans admitted they had been hiding their gifts under "a bushel", and that the gifts were not to be kept to themselves. The Wakandans had no hatred or thoughts of revenge against Europeans and "White America." They understood their own strengths, giftings and their place in the world was for good.

Would Killmonger's vengeance and destruction of the White world have helped change Black communities for the better? NO! Wakandans realized making things better for impoverished communities came from making things better for and in, impoverished communities, not from tearing down and destroying other people, groups and communities.

Chapter 20

CONCLUSION – WE HAVE SINNED

W hile there is no such thing as a Black Church, a White Church or other ethnic Church, we do see divided bodies within "THE CHURCH and continually hear that Sunday morning is "the most segregated hour" in America. What I find troubling is how almost exclusively the fault is assessed against the so-called "White Church." Black and White authors alike have concluded the great divide in today's Church is the fault of white Christians - this is misleading. "THE CHURCH" is segregated primarily because the "Black Church", today, wishes to maintain their heritage. We have bought into the lie, however, (mostly) as a result of "Black Unforgiveness" and "White Guilt."

We are not segregated due to race, rather it is mostly due to language and culture. We have Hispanic churches and churches with separate Hispanic services. Chinese, Hmong, Vietnamese, Russian, Orthodox, and other Christian churches are divided, not necessarily by race, but rather by culture, language, and style. Some baptize by dunking, while others sprinkle; some dance, raise their hands, shout, and run. For many it's piano and organ only. For others it's guitars, trumpets, and drums. Some take communion on the First Sunday, others daily or weekly and – some not at all. Some believe the gifts of the Holy Spirit and miracles still exist today, while others teach miracles were for another dispensation and died with the apostles. When we see a predominantly "White" church, we tend to assume it is due to racism, yet if we see a predominantly Black or other ethnic church, it is due to their language or "style". We say, "they just feel more comfortable in their own culture." Let me say again, I believe we have bought into this thinking (mostly) because of "Black unforgiveness" and "White guilt."

Let me repeat and be very clear, as I know there are those who will say I am denying past injustices, I assure you I am not. However, while it is true Europeans conquered and subjugated natives of other lands for centuries, for millenniums they did that, and worse, to their own. In addition, natives of Africa, Asia and the Americas did no less to their people, in their own lands. Every nation and people group on earth has at one time been enslaved and enslaved others; has attempted to conquer and been conquered by others. Every nation or people has treated others within and without their people group, with brutality incomprehensible to modern thought.

To judge one group, Europeans, aka White people, as the sole or ultimate perpetrators of evil against others, misses the mark by a long shot. It also lets others (US) off the hook, especially when we use the same standard of judgement and stereotyping that we condemn in others. I have tried and sincerely wish to get, particularly Christian believers, to rid themselves of this notion of RACISM. There is no racial problem, the problem is "SIN" –pride, lust and envy all tied up in a neat handy sinful package. Remove the pigment and we still have, as we have seen throughout history, bigotry, discrimination, and prejudice, but for other reasons. Remove race and ethnicity and the fight is over women, land, wealth, or power. Envy, discontentment, yearning, and resentment are the SIN. It began with Cain who killed his brother Abel due to jealousy. Do you think it was about the color of Abel's skin? Wake up brothers and sisters. You have been played for too long.

Many Whites and too many Christians among them, as well as Blacks, have bought into the notion of "White Privilege." "White Privilege" is a close cousin to "White Guilt," which implies, Europeans and their descendants have a natural advantage in life simply because they are born white. What's worse is they are told they should feel badly about this, something they had no control over. This is really off the mark. It is a lie from the "Pit of Hell." It discounts the large number of White children born into poverty and the large and growing number of Black children born into wealth and privilege. For several decades college entrance exams have been skewed and weighted to give extra points to minorities and females. Jobs have been given to less qualified Black and Brown people over more skilled and more qualified Whites. This is not racism, but prejudice and discrimination.

Prejudice is seen as an evil and like anything else can be such. It's like sex. There is healthy and unhealthy sex. There is good and bad power. There are good and bad riches. There are good and bad uses for weapons. One is good and blessed, the other sinful and cursed. Believe it or not prejudice and discrimination are the same. Prejudice can be a useful and positive trait in some cases. The late economist Walter Williams stated, when he chose a wife, he showed prejudice against other women. He discriminated against all others in choosing who would be his life partner. When he chose which university to attend, he displayed prejudice against other institutions of higher learning, and when the school chose him, they discriminated against others. Am I stretching the meaning of these words? Yes, to emphasize my position and expand on the difference between the common and literal use of these two words.

In truth we all have prejudices. In most cases, we choose where to live, what to eat, what to drive, who our friends are and who our life partners will be. We may like blond hair or dark hair, straight or curly; tall or short people, blue eyes, or brown eyes, large breasts or smaller ones, the size of one's rear end, a muscular build or not. These are just a few of the criteria we use to discriminate. Among Black people there was always the "good" hair, the "nappy" hair as well as the paper bag skin complexion comparison. While these are hurtful, it was more about a preference until it was used to elevate one group, demeaning another, within the same race or another. Prejudice can keep young people and all of us out of trouble at times. We can be prejudiced against those who exhibit criminal or other detrimental character. The Bible says, "Bad company corrupts good morals. (1Cor. 15:33) It is not necessarily wrong to choose who we want to be with, we just should not decide to think of ourselves more highly or mistreat those we do not.

I remember watching an infomercial several years ago for "Feed The Children". It featured small rural Appalachian communities in America, verses disadvantaged African children. The narrator made an interesting statement. He said, "You have heard 4 out of 5 children in America go to bed hungry every night. Did you know 3 out of 4 of those children are white?" Man! Talk about opening my eyes. It was kind of like the situation depicted in the book and film, "A Time To Kill," where the lawyer in his closing statement tells the story of a young girl being beaten and abused by a group of white miscreants. The jury, and most of us watching thought he was speaking of a little black girl but in the end he says, "now imagine that the little girl is white." Everyone was instantly jerked awake because they had assumed it was a black girl. It immediately changed people's attitude toward the crime. We have become accustomed to black people, and black children especially, being poor and deprived more than any other ethnic group. However, in the case of athletics and entertainment, it is Black children who seem to have the advantage.

Why do professional football and basketball coaches draft more black than white players? In the NFL 68% of the players identify as Black while 28% identify as White. The NBA numbers are even more slanted. Over 74% of NBA players are black with just over 23% being white. In college basketball, predominantly white schools have all black basketball teams, with the possible exception of one or two white players, who often never or rarely play. We see affirmative action, federal assistance and other programs directed primarily toward minorities, particularly Black minorities. Even at the lower end of the economic scale, I find the idea of "White Privilege" dubious.

I find the idea and promotion of this thinking on "White Privilege" and "White Guilt" especially harmful to the Body of Christ. It fosters a resentment of Whites by non-Whites, while creating a false sense of guilt in Whites. None of this thinking is biblical nor is it helpful. As mentioned earlier, unforgiveness is sin and a major problem which cuts two ways. If Whites cannot forgive themselves, they will overcompensate granting thoughts, ideas, and actions which should not be tolerated. When Blacks fail to forgive Whites, they hold them hostage to things they had nothing to do with and ignore those things they, themselves are responsible for.

Regarding "The Church" today, as stated earlier, it is not divided due to race or racial tensions. It is divided due to cultural differences, yet even today many attribute separate Black and White services to bigotry.

Any number of denominations divide the Catholic, Protestant and Jewish faiths and it is not a big deal. Yet the divide between the Evangelical Church and the so-called Black Church is considered a big deal, and supposed to be all about race. Even Islam, its various streams and varying degrees of belief and practice are not seen to be racially motivated. Are mosques seen as racist for having very few and in most instances no Blacks? How about "The Nation Of Islam", with scarcely a white member, only recently and after very extreme actions, are they seen as racist? Nevertheless, particularly Evangelical Protestantism is considered a bastion of racism.

Generally, Black believers are more prone to react negatively to Whites coming into their world, or to make white visitors feel uncomfortable, than the other way around. I remember becoming a young Evangelical ("Born Again"), Christian, shortly after graduating from college in 1973. I attended Texas Tech University in Lubbock, Texas. Lubbock was still a pretty racially divided city then. They still had a clearly delineated "Black" part of town, "East Lubbock", and a clearly delineated "Mexican" part of town, "North Lubbock." I graduated and left Lubbock that summer and moved to El Paso, Texas, where I met Jesus and changed my life.

That same fall, I returned to Lubbock to evangelize my fraternity brothers and others. I remember one of my fraternity brothers accepting Christ and needing to find a church to plug him into. I had heard about a Trinity Church in Lubbock that was a good church. I looked it up in the "Yellow Pages," and could only find Trinity Baptist Church. I assumed that had to be it. I still vividly remember the day we entered the church. It was 100% elderly white people, and I mean ELDERLY. You could have put a photo of these people in a dictionary, next to the acronym WASP (White Anglo-Saxon Protestant) and you would get the picture. Remembering the stories, I had heard about Whites and "White Church People", especially Baptists, I was apprehensive. I realized it was not the right place but decided to stay anyway. I must tell you though, those people greeted and welcomed us more warmly than many of the "Black churches" I have attended. It was amazing. After the service they almost pleaded with us to return. There were NO other Blacks in the church except for us, two young Black guys with big afros. It was like "Superfly" and "Shaft" were attending their Sunday morning service yet, they were incredibly welcoming.

In El Paso, Texas, I met a girl at the church where I gave my life to Christ. She was white and blond, we became romantically involved and were even considering taking the next step when she left to attend a university north of Dallas. When I visited her, I attended the little

161

country Southern Baptist church she attended, in a rural area north of Dallas. It was a small congregation of maybe 100 people and as an old friend of mine used to say, I was the only "fly in the milk." Needless to say, I raised some eyebrows but, the people were all very friendly. A few months later, my job transferred me to Dallas and while the young lady and I had broken up, I decided to attend that same little church. I attended the church for almost two years before leaving to go to seminary in California. In that entire time, I remained the only "fly in the milk." Nevertheless, no church I have been a part of in my 46 years as a believer was more precious than Shiloh Baptist Church, now Shiloh Church. I grew in the Lord there, and the pastor, who became one of my best friends and mentors, had hoped I would stay and become his assistant. Let me also say it was in this church where my wife and I began our relationship. A relationship which has lasted for 47 years and counting. They recently had a reunion service with as many past and current members coming that could. I was amazed at the change. There were now, white, black, Hispanic, and Asian members, and mixed couples of all kinds and styles. I felt kind of proud to have been a pioneer. Sadly, my dear friend and mentor, John P. Lee, very recently passed away but it was my greatest honor to speak at his funeral.

I share this story, and I have many more, that I won't take up space with, in the US, Europe, Africa and elsewhere. I will simply say, true believers in Christ are not known by their color, sex, or national origin. As scripture says, "by their fruits you will know them." Whenever I hear someone discuss faith and Christianity in terms of race, or any other distinction, I question if they truly know the Author and Finisher of our faith. There is NO distinction in the Church of Jesus Christ. We are all one in Him. If anyone tries to tell you differently walk away. There is One Lord, One faith and One baptism. (Eph. 4:5) - so why should or would we try to make or imply there are divisions.

To my brethren, who are descendants of African slaves, I say forgive and you shall be forgiven.
Trust in the Lord and do good, that you may dwell in the land and live secure. Ps. 37:3 NAB

I have titled this book Y'all Have Sinned, but the reality is, WE have sinned. When Christians point fingers at one another based on race, culture, political or nuances, the enemy wreaks havoc. It is easy for Whites to blame Black people and even easier for Blacks to blame Whites, but are we brothers and sisters in the faith or not? Do you think Islamists care if you are black or white, male, or female, rich or poor, Catholic, Protestant or Pentecostal? Do you think they care if we take communion once a day, once a week or never at all? Do you think they'll inquire if we dunk or sprinkle, use instruments in our worship, sing, traditional or contemporary gospel music? I am sitting here laughing as I write this because these are all real and dividing issues.

Staying with the primary theme of my book, neither white nor black Christians are 100% at fault or 100% guilt free for the state of Black America, or the Church at large. I would say, however, both black and white Christians are 100% at fault for allowing the Church to be in the state it is today; divided and becoming more and more powerless every day. Each of us can say Y'all have sinned yet, in reality, it is WE, who have sinned.

To the white Christian I say yes, some of your predecessors were guilty and complicit in the slavery, abuse and subjection of Black people and people of other races and groups for years. However, many devoted their lives, some even giving their lives to putting an end to the mistreatment of Black Americans and others. Many of the guilty were also guilty of subjection and brutality of poor whites. The Church of Rome became wealthy, powerful, and corrupt, subjecting its members and non-members to horrible abuse for hundreds of years. The Protestant church has been equally guilty in its silence in many ungodly things it overlooked, and in some cases sanctioned in its members.

The history of the Church is not an easy one. In The Crusades, which were wars (mostly justified) against Muslim hordes who were attempting to take over and destroy Christianity and Judaism, man's sinful nature took this to another level turning The Crusades into a grab for land, wealth and power. These wars were followed by many years of fighting and killing among the Catholic and Protestant states. However, like The Crusades, as the fighting evolved it became less about religion and more about wealth, power, land and control. Entire

163

wars were fought over the Christian religion, yet we have been able to get over it and move on. I have yet to see anyone apologize for that, or to see a Catholic Lives Matter movement in Northern Ireland, or a Protestant Lives Matter movement in the South.

We hear how the KKK and southern protestants in the US mistreated Black people, but we forget they also terrorized Catholics, Jews and Republicans who were white. I know I am beginning to beat a dead horse here, but I want to drive home a point. Black Americans do not have a monopoly on suffering, while White Americans and Christians do not have a monopoly on inflicting abuse. We forget it was white Christians who began the push for abolition and equal treatment of ALL people. Many Whites suffered and died for that cause then and during the civil rights movement of the 20th century.

Yes, Y'all have sinned but in reality, WE have ALL sinned!! I say please get over the past sins and mistakes of predecessors on both sides. We are all on the same side and need to unite today more than ever before. Jesus said in Matthew 6:34, "take no thought for tomorrow, for sufficient is the day and the evil thereof." While he spoke of tomorrow or the future, I must exhort you to do the same of the past. Take no thought for the past, for sufficient is today, and the evil thereof. We have enough issues and problems facing us today without worrying or trying to fix the wrongs of the past. As I have tried to show in many ways, every nation, people group and religion, has a history of doing evil to others.

If you are a caring and loving church continue to be a caring, loving church. I find it funny that some of the most giving and caring churches which are already integrated, and involved in ministry in the at risk communities, are the same ones feeling the need to express their "Collective Sin" of the past. Please stop, it is not helpful, it retards your church community and the community you are trying to help and uplift. You are undoing what you propose to do. You chance expressing the "soft bigotry of low expectations", as though those communities are helpless without you, not to mention giving them a reason to reject you. Rise up Church, and demand it of others. Let your answer to "at risk" and lame communities be the same as that of Peter and John as they encountered the lame man at the gate of the temple in Acts 3. "Silver and gold (money & stuff) have we none, but such as we have give we thee. In the name of Jesus of Nazareth, RISE UP AND WALK."

To the Black Christian I say STOP IT!! Stop acting like the plight of the Black community is the fault of whites and especially the "White Church". You wonder why the Nation of Islam gained popularity? It is because you have validated their cry that the "White Christian Devils" caused the ills of the slaves and their descendants. Please stop the nonsense and stop preaching hate, bitterness and unforgiveness. Black communities in America have risen to great heights on their own. Frederick Douglas, Booker T. Washington, Carter G. Woodson, Madame C.J. Walker, and many others showed the way.

I get so tired of hearing that Booker T. Washington talked about picking ourselves up by our bootstraps. Forget bootstraps, that is bunk. What Dr. Washington was saying is, we, as a unit, and united, can lift one another up. Poor Jews, Germans, Italians, Irish, Pols, West Indians, Asians even East and West Africans have come to America, participated in the American Dream and succeeded greatly. Black, West Indians and Africans have come here and thrived. It is only the native born Black Americans, who claim they cannot make it. Booker T. Washington dubbed the Greenwood District of Tulsa the "Black Wall Street." It was ravaged by a white mob and burned in 1921. The other side of the story, which is almost never told, is how they rose to become "Black Wall Street," before and after the riot and fire. Greenwood became more prosperous after the riot than it had been before. Many would now want us to forget THAT history for their own selfish purposes. They want Tulsans and Americans to feel pity and dig into their pockets to throw more good money after bad in the form of "reparations." No one asks the question, what will we do with reparations money if we get it or who is getting most of it. Lawyers, consultants, organizers, many of whom will be white, will get a large percentage of "reparations". It is simple my brethren, as the country song goes, "There Ain't No Future In The Past."

A Dangerous Threat

There are forces at work today trying to destroy faith in Jesus Christ and His Church. Those forces are **atheist/secular humanists, Islamists** and what I call **New Age Syncretizes**.

In the first group are Communists and Socialists who have been bent on destroying Western Civilization for a few hundred years. These people are the modern versions of Marxists/Leninists, and the Fascists and Nazis of the last century. Each of these groups have one thing in common, they were opposed to Judaism and Christianity then and they are opposed to it now. Do not be fooled! Hitler and the Nazis were not Christian, anymore than their cousins, Communists and Socialists. These groups have preyed upon the jealousy and bitterness of the poor and downtrodden, blaming the Christian church, to provoke revolution, to the end of ushering in their godless secular rule. A "rule" which fails to be what they sell it as. We have seen this in nations and within groups who have tried it. It runs contrary to the spirit God placed in mankind. A spirit that yearns to be free, not checked by external forces. Socialism and Communism, while promising a better life for all, has failed to deliver it anywhere it has been tried. Each country or people group who has tried it has said, "we know better than those prior to us and WE can make it work". Nevertheless, they failed like all their predecessors. We would be no different.

Of late we see a fresh attempt to usher in a newer form of socialism called Democratic Socialism. As if adding the word Democratic will make a difference. If the word Democratic meant what they say it means, why was the authoritarian Communist nation of East Germany officially known as the German **Democratic** Republic? Why is North Korea, The **Democratic** People's Party of Korea? Hint, if the name has Democrat or People in it, chances are 9-1 it is neither democratic nor of the people. The Party rules and the Party rules exclusively. You have no rights except those given by the Party. One of, if not, THE first act of these regimes is to remove any knowledge of God or a god from their culture. The next is control over religious expression. The so-called Democratic Socialism which has been tried in Europe for the past 40 to 50 years or so, has been touted as successful by some, and worthy of adoption by America. The reason European and even Chinese Communism appears to have been successful has been the prosperity of America. The freedom and Capitalist system of America and the prosperity that it brings, allows us to buy the products and services other nations provide. Remove the prosperity of America and you remove the prosperity of the world.

Have you ever wondered what happened to the Soviet Communist Party members after the fall of the Iron curtain? It is like they were "Raptured" to use a Christian term. In other words, miraculously and supernaturally taken out of this world. I am afraid not. Most of them went underground and moved west. I often say the best thing that ever happened to the Communist Movement was the fall of the wall. It allowed them to go underground, infiltrate and shape the direction of the institutions of the western world. Our centers of education, universities and even public schools, have had their curriculum affected and turned upside down to where all that was American and good is seen as bad, replaced by a secular and socialist worldview.

The Democrat Party of the United States has adopted this path as the future and is working hard to sell it to Americans. Look at the groups and the manner in which they are manifesting their new direction. Groups like Black Lives Matter, Antifa, and others are exactly who will run this nation if they succeed in implementing their plans. It was the same in each of their predecessors, exploitation throughout those named "Democratic".

A close look at the nations where Socialism and it's more honest but more brutal brothers (Communists) live, will reveal that there is a distinct class difference. Talk about a "good ol' boy network," it does not get any more "good ol' boy" than what you see under Communism. You have the political class, composed of those who rule, the oligarchy composed of businesses that create wealth to keep the political class in power and luxury, and you have the laborers who keep the oligarchs and political class rich and happy. In addition to these, you have the court jester class as I like to call it. These are the athletes and entertainers who dance to the tune of the political class, entertaining and performing for them. The deal is, "make us proud, keep us happy and we will keep you happy. Fail and you can join the rest of the laboring class."

Socialists/Communists are not the only ones at work to undermine the foundation of America.

A second group, Islamists, wish to rid the world of Jews, Christians, and anyone not ready to accept Islamic Sharia law, as the basis for all laws. While they pretend to believe in "prophets" of the Judeo/Christian bible, including Abraham, Moses and Jesus, they reject the central truths of that book in favor of their own. Their main rejection is the divinity and supremacy of Jesus. In their teachings Mohammed was the last and supreme prophet of God, overriding the teachings of all who came before. There are lots of problems with this. The main one bringing their ideology into questions is, while the prior "prophets" all lined up and foretold of the coming of the Messiah, and Jesus was the fulfillment of those prophecies, Mohammed contradicted them. Most notably that Jesus was the Messiah.

Christianity has brought freedom and prosperity everywhere it has flourished; Islam has brought the opposite. Muslims say Jesus was a prophet, and the best one, except for Mohammed as described in the Koran. This is easily debunked by the doctrine of Liar, Lunatic or Lord as put forth from the gospel of John, and made more current by apologists like C.S. Lewis and Josh McDowell. For those unfamiliar with this, it goes as follows. Jesus said he was The Way, The Truth and The Life and NO one gets to heaven except through accepting His blood sacrifice on the cross. He was either who He said he was, the savior and Son of God, or He was a liar or a lunatic. If he was one of the latter, he could not be a good prophet. This by the way debunks the next and last group I want to highlight as well.

There is one other group at work against the Judeo/Christian foundation of America. New Age Syncretism is composed of those who reject any religion as being unique and superior to any other. In other words, there is no single pathway to God or the gods. All roads lead to the same place, we just have to pick and choose "the good" in each and create our own belief system. The problem is they cannot tell you where that "same place" is, because that would make them dogmatic like the other "dogmatic religions." Contrary to this, like it or not, the various faiths are mutually exclusive. Christianity, Islam, and most of the others cannot coexist based on their written doctrines.

What we are seeing in our world today is a uniting of the three belief systems I just outlined vs. a system of belief in the God of Abraham, Isaac and Jacob as seen in Judaism and Christianity. While they are considered two distinct faiths, they are actually one in the same with one separating issue, the Messiah. One believes the Messiah has come in the person of Jesus Christ, while the other still awaits Him. Other than the idea of who Jesus is the faiths are essentially one. While the Jews believe the Messiah is coming, Christians believe it will be the return of the One who came before.

While these anti-Christian/Judaism entities are united now, if they should succeed or come close to succeeding in their quest to eradicate Judeo/Christian thought from the marketplace, they would soon turn on each other like ravenous wolves. An example is the alliance between Stalin and Hitler in the early days of World War II. Stalin and Hitler made a non-aggression pact, which Hitler broke as soon as he thought he was powerful enough to take it all. Russia and Germany each persecuted and killed millions of Jews in their own country, and in countries they occupied. In the same fashion the secular humanist ideologies of socialism and communism would turn on Islam and the New Age syncretists. They currently have one common goal, eradicate Judeo/Christian thought and influence - each is playing a role in that effort. They support each other's causes, and fight against Judeo/Christian influences on culture, while defending each other's right to be an influence. They have taken over the education systems, media, and now wish to take that final step in controlling government.

These are the entities that are behind the various movements that support and control the racial divide in America today. Their plan is to so confuse and cloud the minds of good people that they abandon sound doctrine and policy based upon emotion, guilt and fear. They can be stopped, but we are perilously close to the point of no return.

Rise up, Church, and demand it of others.

I began this book with the story of how God spoke to me a few days before a Shirley Caesar concert in Germany. The message was simple. The descendants of African slaves aka Black Americans have experienced great suffering yet have been greatly blessed with tremendous gifts and favor in the United States of America.

Unfortunately, instead of using these blessings and these gifts to benefit others, we have not only become unforgiving, bitter and resentful, but more covetous, always wanting more and more.

We, as modern-day Josephs should have seen and be seeing our abundant blessings as Joseph did, a gift "to save many people". Many people, especially other people of color around the world look to Black Americans as idols. Black Americans can go to almost any country in the world and are looked upon as "Special". Particularly in Africa our original homeland, where the people are crying out for help. We can do what others cannot and honestly should not have to. To enter into the full blessings of God, I believe we must change the way we think and act.

- First, we must confess the sins of unbelief and unforgiveness. Black believers in Jesus Christ must, like Daniel, confess OUR sins by looking at our lives and realizing how blessed we are, as a group and as individuals. We must confess our ingratitude, for then and only then can we see things in a new light. In a fresh, positive way, full of hope and willingness to work to build a bright future, not only for Black Americans but for all mankind.
- Then, to do the above, we must be ready to FORGIVE! At the end of the Lord's prayer Jesus said the following, "For if you forgive other people when they sin against you, your heavenly Father will also forgive you. But if you do not forgive others their sins, your Father will not forgive your sins." Matthew 6:14-16.
- This is but one piece of scripture that speaks to why we need to forgive. Here are several more:

"Be kind to one another, tender-hearted, forgiving each other, just as God in Christ also has forgiven you." Ephesians 4:32

"Bearing with one another, and forgiving each other, whoever has a complaint against anyone; just as the Lord forgave you, so also should you." Colossians 3:13

"Whenever you stand praying, forgive, if you have anything against anyone, so that your Father who is in heaven will also forgive you your transgressions." Mark 11:35

"Be on your guard! If your brother sins, rebuke him; and if he repents, forgive him." Luke 17:3

"And if he sins against you seven times a day, and returns to you seven times, saying, 'I repent', forgive him." Luke 17:4

I think it is clear, that God is serious about forgiveness. Let us then forgive AND forget, because in the forgetting is the forgiveness.

When I speak of forgiveness, I am also speaking to my melanin challenged (WHITE) brethren saying, please, please, please, forgive yourselves and your forefathers. Forgive and be forgiven. How is it we can believe God forgives all our and other people's current sins and yet not forgive our forefathers for theirs? It is like oops, God missed those sins, so we need to hold them against others. He can forgive theft, adultery, murder, and all manner of sin, but slavery and prejudice, those must have shown up on the seventh day when God was resting. Those cannot be forgiven and we must hold on to those forever. If you do not forgive, you will be trapped forever under a cloud of guilt and in UNBELIEF, saying this is too big for GOD. It is, of course, not and therefore, if God forgives and removes this stain, we MUST do no less.

Most believers have heard the story of the song, "Amazing Grace." How the author of the song, John Newton, had been captain of a slave ship for many years, transporting hundreds of slaves across the Atlantic, yet he found forgiveness. If he could find it, who are we not to forgive and receive it.

I cannot stress enough the importance of forgiveness. Forgiving others and forgiving ourselves. As part of forgiveness, we must let go of any and all bitterness:

Pursue peace with all people, and holiness, without which no one will see the Lord. Looking carefully lest anyone fall short of the grace of God; lest any root of bitterness springing up cause trouble, and by this many become defiled." Hebrews 12:14-15

171

If you wonder whether you have forgiven someone, just ask yourself if you have any bitterness toward them and if so, why.

Just as God asked me to do 48 years ago when I received Him, we must let it go. The root of bitterness will destroy any and all good in our lives. Unforgiveness and the bitterness that comes from it will cloud all we see. We will never be able to receive God's blessings. Once we forgive others and/or ourselves, I pray our eyes will open to see how blessed and fortunate we are - and the greater need of others around the world. It is my prayer that the descendants of African slaves, can one day do as Joseph did; see and say to our African family AND our fellow European descendant citizens:

"But as for you, you meant evil against me; but God meant it for good, in order to bring it about as it is this day, to save many people." Gen. 50:20 NKJV

Black Americans, with the help of others, can affect change, not only in in Africa and other places around the world as no one else can, but the change we make here at home is the single greatest thing we can do. I hope this is only the beginning of the journey for many. It will take faith and trust to see it through BUT I promise it will be worth it.

In closing I want you to keep this in your heart, but please "Pass It On". There is a 60s/70s Jesus People song that many (older folks) may remember. It goes as follows.

It only takes a spark to get a fire going
And soon all those around
Can warm up in its glowing
That's how it is with God's Love
Once you've experienced it
You spread His love to everyone
You want to pass it on.
I wish for you my friend
This happiness that I've found
You can depend on Him
It matters not where you're bound

I'll shout it from the mountain top
I want my world to know
The Lord of love has come to me
I want to pass it on
Pass It On- Kurt Kaiser- 1969

ABOUT THE AUTHOR

E ddie Huff was born to a single German mother and a black American (GI) father, in post World War 2 Germany. He grew up between 2 worlds, at first in a small German village speaking only German. From this world, at the age of 7, he was transplanted to a completely different world, that of the projects of Philadelphia. Growing up as a Black American child in the 60s Eddie would move back and forth from predominantly black environments to very integrated ones. He has, however, always considered himself Black and counts it as a supreme privilege to share in that rich history.

As a freshman at Texas Tech University he became a "Black Radical/Hippie" accepting all of the late 60s early 70s Leftist ideology. He became vice president of the Black Student Union at Texas Tech as well as president of the charter chapter of Alpha Phi Alpha fraternity while there. It was not until his of accepting Jesus Christ as his personal savior in El Paso, Texas, one month after his graduation that Eddie began to see the world in a new way and begin on a new path with a new vision.

Eddie Graduated from Texas Tech with a B BA in management and attended Melodyland School of Theology in Anaheim, CA, in their M. Div. program. He is a licensed minister.

From 1981 to 1992 Eddie with his wife Vickie and 4 children served as missionaries with Youth With A Mission (YWAM). Eddie was director of Musicians for Missions, a division of YWAM in Amsterdam, Holland from 1981-84, then became director of the Augsburg, Germany YWAM base, leading Discipleship Training Schools and directing a Christian book distribution center providing Christian books and music to the U.S. Military throughout Europe and the Middle East. In addition to these duties Eddie spent extensive time in Uganda, Kenya and South Africa leading teams doing relief work, and teaching for Youth With A Mission bases there.

In his service with Youth With A Mission and beyond, Eddie has spoken before thousands in Europe and Africa, and the United States. In addition to this he was one of the main promoters of Christian and Gospel concerts and tours for American artists throughout Europe.

In 1992 Eddie and family returned to the U.S. where he has been an insurance agent and financial services rep. with his own agency. He is a public speaker and former owner of a gospel recording label. For 6 years he was also co-host of a top, Local Talk Radio program in Tulsa and has written hundreds of articles on public policy, socio-political, and spiritual themes.

This is Eddie's first book and has been 30 years in the making.

THE EMANCIPATION OF UNCLE TOM

O ne of the saddest things I have encountered in looking into the history of the "Black Community" is the defiling of the name "Uncle Tom." For the very rare individual that may never have heard of or understood the significance of "Uncle Tom", let's take a stroll back in history.

"Uncle Tom's Cabin" was a fictional novel written by a lady named Harriet Beecher Stowe and published in 1852.

The name Uncle Tom has been turned into a term and classification over the last 150 years or so, now seen as pejorative against a black person, particularly males, deemed a race traitor. This is far from the intent of the author.

Stowe came from a very religious family, the daughter of a Calvinist preacher. This makes for an interesting story in itself in that Calvinists believed in predestination, and as such should have believed that those born into servitude were there because of God's will. This was the idea behind South African, Calvinists of the Dutch Reformed Church that ushered in Apartheid a century later. In spite of this, Stowe became a staunch abolitionist and was inspired to write the book that many said led to the Civil War and many credit with beginning the end of slavery in America. The book sold 300,000 copies in the US and over 1,000,000 copies in Great Britain within its first few years.

The story told of a southern plantation owned by a brutal and despicable man named Simon Legree, his overseers, and a hand full of slaves, of which the central character, Tom was one. Tom was a very faithful slave who loved God and lived it. He suffered much under Simon Legree, and his black overseers, "Sambo and Quimbo." Sambo and Quimbo regularly beat Tom and other slaves at the direction of Simon Legree. In the end Tom sacrificed his own life for his fellow slaves, being beaten to death by Simon Legree after he helped a female slave escape and would not reveal her whereabouts.

While the brutality and the treatment of the character, Uncle Tom, was painful to read about, I feel the brutality, treatment and misrepresentation of the character in the real world, particularly by those who should know better, has been even worse. "Uncle Tom" was a Christ figure laying down his own life for his friends and fellow slaves. He was not a weak character; he was a strong and noble character whose name and depiction have been grossly altered by those with their own ulterior motives. Since after the Civil War, the name or dubious title of "Uncle Tom," has been used to attack black people who choose to go against the grain. Instead of recognizing that the character gave his life to fight the evil Simon Legree for the freedom of his fellow slaves. You would think he was the overseer working to keep his fellow slaves bound and in servitude.

I believe roles have been intended to be totally reversed by despicable individuals and groups, but the so-called "Uncle Tom's" today are actually much like the character "Uncle Tom," fighting to free their people from the racist, mostly Democrat and Progressive plantations. Those who attack the various voices of freedom and independent thought are the real villains and are the modern day "Sambos and Quimbos."

The "Sambos and Quimbos" of today have been left unchallenged for too long. It is time they are called out and confronted as the real enemies of their people. We find them in leadership roles in churches, in political offices, in higher education, and in the media. They are easy to recognize. Just like the overseers "Sambo and Quimbo," they would be the ones attacking any black person who would dare choose to have the audacity to be a Conservative, a Republican, or question what the Democrat and Progressive masters say is allowed for us to think. It is time to emancipate Uncle Tom. We need to set him free and bestow upon him honor long overdue.

Whether it is truth or legend, that Abraham Lincoln said upon meeting Harriet Beecher Stowe, "so this is the little lady who started this great war." It is very likely true that the book "Uncle Tom's Cabin" so pricked the conscience of half the nation that it led to the great war and freedom for the descendants of African slaves in the United States of America.

BIBLIOGRAPHY

Chapter 4

1 - https://www.pbs.org/wgbh/evolution/darwin/nameof/index.html

2 - http://eugenicsarchive.ca/discover/tree/523377f35c2ec50000000050

3 - The Big Lie: Die Zeit Ohne Beispiel- Joseph Goebbels; January 12, 1941, pp. 364-369; Zentral Verlag Der NDSP

Chapter 7

1 - Albania, The First Atheist State; Robert Royal- Arlington Ctholic Herald (2000)

2 - https://face2faceafrica.com/article/slavery-africa-today

Chapter 8

1-https://iowaculture.gov/sites/default/files/history-education-pss-are-construction-atlanta-Transcription.pdf

Chapter 9

1 - https://www.blackpast.org/african-american-history/1865-frederick-douglasswhat-black-man-wants/

2 - http://www.emersonkent.com/speeches/harvard_university_address_washington.htm

Chapter 10

1 - Booker T. Washington- Up from slavery; Chapter 1, P.4; Public domain.
https://www.slps.org/cms/lib/MO01001157/Centricity/Domain/10749/UpFromSlavery1-4.pdf

2 - https://iowaculture.gov/sites/default/files/history-education-pss-are-construction-Atlanta-transcription.pdf

3 - William H. Taft - Condolence letter to Booker T. Washington family.

Chapter 11

1 - Mararet Sanger "Letter to Dr. Clarence J. Gamble; Page 2; December 10, 1939
https://libex.smith.edu/omeka/files/original/
d6358bc3053c93183295bf2df1c0c931.pdf

Chapter 13

1 - Nation Of Islam Website; https://www.noi.org/noi-history/
2 - https://www.christianpost.com/news/louis-farrakhan-urges-crowd-to-kill-Those-Who-kill-us-calls-for-retaliation-in-speech-at-baptist-church.html
3 - https://new.finalcall.com/2013/05/23/national-geographic-proves-Teaching-onmr-yakub/

Chapter 14

1 - Gunfight: The Battle Over The Right To Bear Arms; September 19th 2011 by W. W. Norton Company
2 - Ibid
3 - https://www.marxists.org/history/usa/workers/black-panthers/1966/10/15.htm

Chapter 15

1 - Cornel West- "The Radical King"; "The Radical King" - Beacon Press; Boston Ma 1992 https://www.inspiringquotes.us/author/8182-cornel-west/about-commitment
2 - https://kinginstitute.stanford.edu/king-papers/documents/autobiography religious-development
3 - http://mlk-kpp01.stanford.edu/kingweb/publications/papers/vol1/501122-An_Autobiography_of_Religious_Development.htm

Chapter 16

1 - Document 17B: W. E. B. Du Bois, "Black Folk and Birth Control," Birth Control Review, 16, no. 6 (June 1932): 166-67; https://documents.alexanderstreet.com/d/1000670632

2 - Mararet Sanger "Letter to Dr. Clarence J. Gamble"; Page 2; December 10, 1939
https://libex.smith.edu/omeka/files/original/
    d6358bc3053c93183295bf2df1c0c931.pdf

Chapter 17

1 - https://www.nopactalent.com/speaker/tim-wise.php

2 - http://www.timwise.org/2010/09/oh-surprise-dinesh-dsouza-like-all-right-wingers-isa-liar/

3 - https://www.npr.org/2020/06/03/869071246/how-white-parents-can-talk-to-their-Kids-about-race P. 139 4321

Chapter 20

1 - https://lyricstranslate.com/en/kurt-kaiser-pass-it-lyrics.html